THE TIGER, THE LIZARD AND ORSON WELLES

Ann Rye

Published in 2015 by Creative Print Publishing Ltd

Copyright © 2015 Ann Rye

The right of Ann Rye to be identified as the author of this work has been asserted in accordance with the Copyright, Designs and Patents Act 1988.

All rights reserved. No reproduction, copy or transmission of this publication may be made without written permission. No paragraph of this publication may be reproduced, copied or transmitted save with the written permission or in accordance with the provisions of the Copyright Act 1956 (as amended.) Any person who does any unauthorised act in relation to this publication may be liable to criminal prosecution and civil claims for damage.

Paperback ISBN 978-1-909049-30-7

For *GEORGE and LOUIS*

From *Granny Anny with love.*

My gratitude to *VANESSA ROSENTHAL* for her invaluable help and support. To my son James and my dear friends for their love and encouragement.

My thanks to cousin Carl Pettman for sharing excerpts of his grandfather's – Uncle Albert's – journals from H.M.S. Manxman.

Mother as Floradora

These memories are from before, during and after a long life in the acting profession; the interesting people – and animals, as the title indicates – that I have encountered and known and loved.

The letter read: Dear Ms. Rye, would you mind working with a tiger as the leopard is not available. No, of course I didn't mind, and the letter is under "treasures" in the memory. The show was an episode of SEXTON BLAKE, made in the '60s, with that adorable actor, Lawrence Payne.

The tiger belonged to the Chipperfield family, one of whom was in attendance throughout the shoot. My character was a gun-carrying German Baroness, therefore, of course, a bit of a baddie! My pet tiger was called Putzi and he was a very nice tiger person. Even tempered, loved his head being stroked, as most cats do, and didn't mind being on the end of a lead while the Baroness had him accompany her everywhere.

Trouble, not of "Putzi's" doing, came before one of our entrances into the baronial hall's drawing room. The double doors would be flung open by a couple of flunkeys from inside and in we'd go. Unfortunately, the doors opened outwards, in other words, at us, or more specifically, at Putzi, who was lying patiently waiting to be guided through. Every time the cue for the doors to open came and action was shouted, the doors thumped Putzi on the nose. He was so polite about this repeated battering – nothing is ever just right the first time on film. If only I had been able to persuade him to stand up before our entrance, all these slights to his dignity and his nose could have been avoided but on the sixth time he'd had enough. He burst through the doors with me hanging on to his lead until his strength was greater than mine. He galloped all over the set, desperately trying to get away from this unnatural and claustrophobic atmosphere.

After what seemed like an age, Putzi's owner/trainer appeared and after he had taken a flying leap at a flat – a pretend wall, in which the fireplace resided – he found that too was unreal as it gave way under his weight and it was then that Ms. Chipperfield was able to catch him All the men reappeared from the safe distances to which they had repaired and we carried on with the scene.

My most vivid memory of the incident is of my dresser, climbing at a rate of knots, up the iron fire-escape ladder. I actually don't remember ever seeing her again, though I suppose I must have done!

In the cast list, Putzi was listed as Kuma.

As soon as the scene was over and Kuma had been taken out, I knocked on Lawrence Payne's dressing room door. I had worked with him before and knew he was as caring about animals as I am. I asked him would he have a word with the producers about not using this poor animal in such a confined space and if necessary, to film him separately, out of doors, where he was happier. Lawrence was entirely in agreement and as the responsible Leading Man, in true Sexton Blake style dealt with all problems.

A much more recent invitation to work with someone in addition to human beings was without prior warning, really.

I had seen that there was a pet lizard mentioned in the

script and I wondered how on earth a lizard could be prevented from darting about all over the place in order to be filmed. After arriving at the usual ungodly hour for make-up and wardrobe in a small bedroom at a large rambling old farm house, I went down on to the set – a small, homely-looking sitting room with a two-seater settee facing a wood-burning fire, and two armchairs either side of it. The director greeted me while lighting was being set up and told me I would be sitting on the settee doing the crossword and the lizard would be sitting beside me. Still puzzling over the feasibility of this, I nevertheless sat down, picked up the rather tatty looking tabloid whose crossword my character was to tackle and ran over my lines in my head, for use later with human actors. The room went quiet and people removed themselves and all was cleared ready for rehearsal, followed by shooting . There were some expletives coming from the connecting door behind me and the sound of it banging shut. I looked round to see who had entered and there was my lizard, all five feet two inches of him, being carried rather awkwardly towards his seat on the sofa beside me. His "trainer" (how do you *train* a giant lizard called an Iguana?)

plonked him down unceremoniously beside me, manhandling him somewhat in an effort to persuade him to stay put. The Iguana's expression looked to me as though he was in total disbelief about what was happening to him. He started heavily breathing through an enormous mouth with a long and rather active tongue. He turned to face me – God knows how I appeared to him – and he stayed staring at me throughout the scene. I tried to get into acting mode. Sitting on a sofa, in front of a roaring fire, reading a newspaper? Nothing to it. Start now and you'll be ready for *ACTION* when it comes. I, who want to love all creatures, was trying very hard not to avert my eyes from the newspaper to the open-mouthed creature beside me, but you have to look, don't you? Whenever I did, there he was, staring in my direction at me wondering, I suppose, who the hell I was, as I was wanting to ask him what my approach to him should be. This isn't a *usual* pet. Does he want to be talked to, stroked, patted on the head? Not to try and find out, I thought. His body seemed to extend fulsomely into his tail which was made for lashing rather than wagging or even waving like a cross cat. No, here was a fellow-artiste well outside my experience, in very close proximity, with no lines and a *totally committed stare through revolving eyes.*

In a later scene the creature had been placed in my character's armchair, facing the fire. I had to enter with my supper tray and the intention to sit in my chair and enjoy a nice fireside supper. My line to "Iggy" was: "Ger off you daft bugger!" and then persuade him to do just that. No, he was happy sitting in my chair thank you and wasn't going to move. The camera was running while all this went on – very amusing for those watching the monitor in the next room, but a battle of wills between me and an Iguana. I put my supper tray down on the little table beside the armchair and approached Iggy with both hands free to lift, push or pull him on to the floor – which seemed a bit mean anyway – after all, he was there first. All my attempts failed and eventually and to hell with the camera running, I shouted for the so-called "keeper" and asked him how to persuade my character's "pet lizard" to move. "Oh, you just lift his tail and tickle him under there . . ." I thought, and said, that this seemed a dreadful liberty, it was a very private place, that it was too intrusive and I wasn't keen to do it. The Keeper removed himself from the room and, praying that boldness – and the Iguana – would be my friend, I held his heavy tail up and with the other hand, gave him a hard tickle. He just turned and looked at me, as though thinking *what the hell does she think she's doing?* I breathed deeply and had another go, easing myself into a position where I might slide into the chair and displace him. It worked! He slithered down between my knees, lay down there for a minute or so, then lurched towards the fireplace, stretched himself out and stayed there for the rest of the scene, very relaxed and no threat to the rest of "my family" of highly suspicious and apprehensive husband and sons when they entered and took their seats.

I dwelt on these two creatures because in real life I'd never have known such an association. There is a kind of nobility about each and I feel privileged to have had this closeness.

There were once two beautiful bloodhounds, ever sad-looking as we expect them to look, that belonged to my character and with whom I had a joyous time working. They were offered to me as a gift by the trainer/owner because we had got on so well. Such is the unreliability of the location of life in our business, I sadly declined. I hope they both had a good life and gave as much pleasure to someone else as they gave to me.

Mind you, it's not always a pleasure. Animals are unnaturally subdued or suspicious when they're required to behave in a certain way in our medium and an Alsatian in my charge, in a series about vets, was totally resigned to having a miserable time. Because of his "accident" in the story he was covered with sticky stage blood, which is coloured glycerine and which had to be regularly re-applied, so that his coat was revolting to the touch and very, very uncomfortable for him. No amount of gentle talk and cajoling could arouse any reaction from him and, as usual, the scene was repeated several times and then the location would change, so he had to be heaved off the vet/actor's examination table. Poor old boy. He stays in my mind with anxious memories. The owner had a large collection of "stage animals" and I hoped they were not all as unhappy as this dog, but I fear they probably were.

Feed The Nation

Where did it start, this love? I think it I must have been very young when all children of my age and thereabouts were evacuated from the South-East coast of England because Hitler's armies were expected to turn up on the French side and of course, did, poised to invade. I was, I suppose, a lonely only child. Never felt lonely, but that may well be because of the enormous consolations. There were visiting kittens, dogs, horses, cows, pigs and one very affectionate toad and chickens, rabbits and guinea pigs. I was profoundly happy. Innocent of what might and did happen to many of these creatures. After all, small farmers like my Father, were depended upon to feed the country but despite the fears and the hard-working life, it was indeed a good life.

Memories have become old friends; vignettes from the forties, and are amongst the treats of memory. There are, of course, tricks. Things you can't remember or half-remember and which you embellish as though you have to complete if not perfect a story so that it can sit comfortably in the memory bank.

Spitfires and Dogfights

In the drowsy haze of a summer's day the dog fighters are at it again and I am re-living the battle for the skies of 1940, mesmerized by the speed and agility of the Spitfires and the doggedness of the Messerschmidts who could take only last-minute evasive action – last minute because as we all know now, they just didn't have the speed if they saw a Spitfire, to avoid it. Every now and then one of theirs would plummet from the sky, in flames. No time to open a parachute. When the bits of the bodies, the foreign bodies at any rate, were later retrieved they wouldn't be considered one of us. Their bits would be buried outside the churchyard.

This last memory stays with me particularly. "*Outside* the churchyard". I can see the narrow strip of grass, once a footpath, unkempt, with unmarked crosses as the only reminder of these brave but *foreign* lads.

Despite our lightning speed, *ours* too were shot down by *theirs*. There were lucky moments when pilots had been able to bale out and open their 'chutes, but some were already on fire and would never meet the ground gently enough to survive. In any case – and this is another memory that perturbs me greatly - one of *theirs* would randomly polish them off with a spray of bullets as he floated rapidly downwards. I daresay we did it to them, but at that time, *they* were the evil ones.

If we children were lucky, and that's how we thought of it, we could run like hell, beat the officials to it and find a fallen Spitfire. If it had only done a gentle nose-dive it was sufficiently intact for us to climb into its cockpit which was smaller than we thought, but with soft leather comfort, still warm as often as not, where the hapless pilot had so recently sat. If it was badly damaged, we'd retrieve as much shrapnel as our pockets would hold and run all the way home. Innocent children with their secrets and their spoils of war-play.

Now I'm not so brave. If an aircraft engine is making an unfamiliar noise, I imagine that it will crash and I will not have the courage to run towards it to see if I can help. In my mind I will run away and that makes me feel rather ashamed.

This is an often repeated nightmare. Is that really how I wanted to behave *then?* Was I more afraid of not joining the big boys who had accepted me as one of them, a mad daredevil with pigtails flying, or was I running my engine on pure adrenalin as so many were.

Well, telling the tale now, as it really was to a five-year-old then, is at once a relief and also the reliving of a time when fear was part of you. The heaviness of it was always there. The long Summer days had thunderstorms too and my Mother used to say that's God, having the last word. A good old-fashioned snub to them and I found that a comfort. While a storm was raging the war machines wouldn't. I believed that. Another scene, incidental to the battles above, was the delight some of theirs took in machine gunning anything or anyone that moved beneath them. One flew low over my father as he was picking fruit from a pear tree and showered the tree next to him so that it split in two. Clever really. It became a dining-out story and after the customary Sunday afternoon tea, when the guests would be shown round the plantation, the flower garden and the orchards, the tree had to be inspected at close quarters with many oohs and aaahs and goodness mes. People didn't say fuckin-ell in those days. I remember my Mother heard a man on a bicycle say it as he was riding past and, firmly taking my hand, she took me to find my Father and she asked him what it was the man was saying and just what did it mean. I don't remember the answer. To the young and pure all things are pure.

Rural life in those days remained idyllic, despite the war.

Sunday Teas

Sunday tea was a splendid and regular ritual. I particularly loved going to the Bassetts. Tea, I should explain, was a cross between afternoon tea and high tea. Sandwiches neatly arranged on china plates, sometimes made with lettuce, which when very young I called cabbage. For years afterwards, a sandwich with lettuce was always a cabbage sandwich in our house. Then there would be cucumber, tomato and ham, chicken and turkey sandwiches, in season; all home grown and reared. The slices of bread were the thinnest I have ever seen, cut by Nelly, the deaf sister, at the scrubbed-white kitchen table with what seemed to be a dangerously sharp knife. Sandwiches were followed by home-made scones with farm butter. Scone-making was a competition which all our friends joined. Who's were the best? Sometimes my mother's, sometimes Rhoda's, sometimes my father's – never Aunty Ida's. More of her later. Then came the beautifully made sponges, the buns and the rock cakes. All the while tea was being poured from a silver teapot, accompanied by a silver hot water jug and a silver milk jug. The china service was Royal Albert. Very decorative. The fruit cake was left on its stand, later to be accompanied by a glass of port, but uncut for the next hour or so.

The two Bassett sisters, spinster ladies, Nelly and Rhoda, had each lost a loved one in WWI. Such kind and gentle creatures and what they didn't know about growing things certainly wasn't worth knowing. They had a lovely sense of humour and, remembering them now, I wonder how they disguised the heavy sadness of loving and losing. Sometimes their brother, Edwin, who was the village blacksmith, joined us. Another occasional and delightful guest-refugee from London was Mrs. Mitchie. She really should have been on the stage; she loved telling tales and having us all wrapt by hearing what she said in a rich, gravely voice. I miss characters like her even now; and she was a kind person, loved children. Edwin Bassett, on the other hand, was a man of few words but silent memories of wartime horrors. Anyway, the ritual was tea, then the perambulation.

I think it was William Barnes, a contemporary of Thomas

Hardy, deserving of wider recognition in my view, who had enjoyed similar after-tea times. Trouble is, he wrote in Dorsetshire dialect but nevertheless, the description in his poetry echoes my memories of the walks round the market gardens of friends, commenting on progress, praising the tomatoes and the runner beans, and the fruit-laden trees, sympathizing with weather-damage and stopping to give carrots to the Shire horse – a gentle, hardworking creature and a sine qua non in those days. There was usually a dog or so accompanying the party and often a cat or two. Inspection was open to all.

It seems to me now that domestic animals had much greater freedom then. People didn't worry about their paws carrying disease or their poo getting on the hands of kids. Children would have been told from the cradle probably only once – . that picking up dog poo was forbidden because it was messy and might be poisonous. If you trod in it, you were to wipe your shoe in the grass and wash it in the stream. It would have seemed eccentric, to say the least, for people to be picking up excretia in little pre-plastic bags. Horse dung, of course, was a valued commodity and men used to drive wagon-loads of it through the streets of villages and towns – anywhere where there might be a garden in need of fertilization – particularly a rose garden. Now, the prevailing practice is to buy bags of chemically treated stuff, at considerable expense which, I suppose, is just as well because there are so few working horses.

Harking back to times which it is tempting to think were so much better than the *now,* is subject to a post-editing process which is really quite clever. The bad things either disappear or acquire some humorous aspects.

Fear is less fearful, rape, dare I say it, wasn't always rape? Love, undoubtedly, seemed more intense.

It is important to me to remember people like the Peppers and they deserve more than a thumb-nail sketch. There was such richness in their characters, such strength and they showed such generosity of spirit to us. I say "to us" advisedly as you will understand when we pass the rose gardens. I doubt if there's a couple like them anywhere in

Britain to-day. He looked like Gladstone and she . . . no description can do her justice. She and he probably had only a couple of teeth between them, so her wizened look was partly due to sunken cheeks, empty of teeth and partly due to digging up potatoes, strawberry picking, weeding, pruning, clearing out the stable . . . the list is almost endless.

She and Mr. Pepper – we never knew his Christian name – it was always that, not the *forename* of today -and my Father had known the couple all his life. To them he remained a boy and respect in all its guises, was de rigueur.

The farmhouse was called *The Grove* probably because Poplars had once bordered the fields either side of the lane leading to a copse in which the house was half hidden, but the Poplars had become more sparse so when the copse came into view you could see why the house was called *The Grove*. It was a sprawling house, originally Tudor, but with many additions and alterations over the years, nestled in amongst trees of all kinds. The Yew on the lawn opposite being the tallest and probably the oldest. The lane turned left at the house. There were two rose gardens, one in front of the house and one opposite, the other side of the lane.

When I referred to The Peppers generosity of spirit, I recall a tale which would rather contradict that. I remember her telling us, many a time, egged on by my Father, about the time when she entered the bedroom and caught the maid leaning out of the window, chatting to her boyfriend. "I never 'esitated", she said, "I went up be'ind her and pushed her out the window!" She said this last bit triumphantly and if anyone expressed concern she would tell them it was all right, the silly girl had fallen in the bushes and she wouldn't be making eyes at her boyfriend again in a hurry.

I still hope that the *bushes* were not the rose bushes. When we arrived we would usually enter by the back door, which was actually to the side of the house. There was an entrance lobby then a step down into a vast flagstoned kitchen with a big, black cooking range, a kettle permanently steaming on top of it and an enormous kitchen/dining table, regularly scrubbed. It needed to be – I vividly remember the old girl making pastry on it, for a pie to be enjoyed by us all later. Accompanying Mrs. Pepper on the table and enjoying the rich pickings, was one of the hens, *co-errrrking* happily as it carefully lifted one leg at a time, as they do, ignored by the old girl until it got too close to the rolling process, then she saw it off with a threatening wave of the rolling-pin and an expletive. The hen stayed in the kitchen and obviously thought of itself as a friend of the family, with the occasional blip in the relationship with its mistress.

Later, as we tucked into the apple pie, it never occurred to me to worry about what little gift from the hen might have got into the pastry. *You've got to eat a peck of dirt before you die.* was the philosophic expression then, adhered to by most!

Tea at the Peppers was a little less refined than at the Bassetts, earlier described. The bread was more roughly cut and the jam pots would be on the table, rather than in dishes matching the tea-set. Always, on these occasions, Tom Palmer, the Peppers' right-hand man, would limp into the room, pull up a chair and almost immediately become the life and soul of the party. No-one ever mentioned how his leg was injured and he must have been in a fair bit of pain. It may have been another ghastly threshing machine incident, which, on separate occasions, got rid of my paternal Grandfather's eye and cousin Teddy's leg. Nevertheless, Tom Palmer's aim in life was to tell stories, fact-based from within a small radius between the Farm and the village church but with a fair bit of dramatic licence. Tom Palmer was the equivalent, I suppose, of a farm manager nowadays. He loved his work and he was utterly loyal to his employers, the Peppers. He was treated as one of the family. He was never called just Tom, always Tom Palmer, as though the names were hyphenated.

The meal would eventually reach the apple pie stage and would be eaten with relish and nobody died. The fruit cake would be put on a tray with the bottle of Port and glasses and taken into the drawing room which, considering the appearance of the Peppers and Tom Palmer, was palatial. A beautiful carpet, generous fireplace, mahogany furniture, a couple of chaises longues and two or three well upholstered armchairs with velvet covers. The overall impression of the room was of rich maroon.

Before we moved on to the drawing room, we had to follow the usual pattern – round the estate to compare notes. I loved this bit the most because I could skip ahead up the lane, which had turned into a wide tractor path, by myself, while the grown-ups talked of poor returns on some vegetables sent to market and good returns on others. My first *friend* would be a Golden Retriever in his kennel at the side of the lane. I wasn't supposed to touch him because apparently he'd bitten someone. Well he didn't bite me and who can blame him, tied to a post outside a kennel day in, day out. Next, on the right and set back across the grass, was the stable in which the enormous white/grey shire horse lived. He was a working boy called Prince – a very common name for horses then, presumably after the darling of many, the Prince of Wales! Prince and I had what I can only describe as a love affair without sex. *Someone much later in my life once described a close friendship with him as that.* I kissed Prince and cuddled him and brushed him and on more than one occasion, lay down in the straw beside him and pretended to be asleep. He responded, it seemed to me, with equal devotion and great care to avoid any clumsiness that might occur because of the enormous difference in our sizes.

My time with Prince usually ended just as *they* were returning from the top orchard and ready to go through the wrought-iron gate in the wall into *Paradise Garden.* That wasn't what they called it but when I was quite young I heard Delius's music for the first time and then, and ever since, the music will take me to that very special *paradise.*

Once through the gate, a grass path stretched straight in front of you, past numerous clumps of rhubarb and several acres of cherry trees on the right. Sweet cherries for the market – and us - and Morello, sour cherries for cherry brandy - this a great favourite, kept in large stone jars for at least a year and then . . . Watch out!

Once, my Father and his friends had formed a band and they called themselves *The Raggle Taggle Gypsies* – everyone knew that song in those days. Anyway, the band needed somewhere to practise as they were turned down; in some quarters - indeed, turned *out.* Will, my Father, asked the Peppers if they could have a spot on their land in order to practice for the next dance. The purpose of playing at these dances was to raise money for a new village hall – which was built within five years much to my Father's and Mother's great pride. Both Peppers agreed that the band could practise in the Cherry orchard as they would make more than enough noise to scare the birds away from the cherries.

On the left hand side of the long grass path was a profusion of colour. Not orderly, like in most Stately Home gardens, but as though everything had appeared without invitation and showed itself to best advantage. When Winter came the evergreen shrubs held the border fort until the colours came again. All these growing delights were sheltered by the tall and ancient brick wall, which went all round this *paradise garden* and against which grew Cox's apples, peaches and even some apricots. Roses climbed between them where space permitted and added to the colour and the scent. A rather strange sight would sometimes emerge at the back of the cherry orchard from a large rotunda, built of bricks but painted black, with tiny windows and a front door. The building was completely out of place but somehow added to the mystery of the area. One day, a strange man, darkly and shabbily dressed, opened the door just as we were coming to the end of the grass path. He stopped and stared at us without waving or smiling. I don't remember being frightened of him, he looked bewildered and could even have been the apparition of a dream. That, I was told later, was Rumble. *Rumble?* As with Tom Palmer's presence in the Peppers' lives, Rumble's was also taken for granted and no-one ever questioned it. He never called at the house but I remember some time later seeing him with a scythe in his hand, rhythmically cutting the grass away from the base of the Victoria plum trees. Was he shell-shocked from the First World War, the unfortunate child of brother and sister – there was a lot of that about then – or just one of life's eccentrics? Was he happy? I wondered.

After the oohs and aahs and tastes of any ripe fruit, my Mother would always be presented with a bag or two of cherries or peaches or whatever was ready to be eaten. Then the Walk Through Paradise Garden would be over and we'd walk back up the long green path, out through the iron gate and back on to the track which would take us to the house again. I would have one more visit to Prince.

Back at the house, we would be ushered into the drawing room and *She* would start to pour the wine, which would sometimes be Cherry Brandy, depending on its readiness, in a break with tradition from Port. Tom Palmer would pass the glasses round to each of us while Mrs. Pepper cut the scrumptious fruit-cake.

The grate would be full of logs and Tom Palmer would start the fire, which would soon be ablaze. He was very good at that. He would almost always then sit down on the sofa beside my Mother. She did her best, bless her, but having been told – by the man himself, I think – that he sewed himself into his underwear at the beginning of Winter and only removed it once May was out – blossom or month, I have never known which, my Mother started to feel uncomfortable and after the customary toasts and munching of *excellent* fruit cake, Will would announce our departure and off we would go.

Unhappily, almost always the first thing that had to happen when we got home, was that my Mother had to get rid of the fleas which seemed to find her alone, an attractive proposition. My Father would strip the double bed and she would remove her clothes and lie on the white linen sheets so that the little blighters could be seen and, with rapid finger agility, caught. She would immediately get into a hot bath and her clothes and the bedclothes, would be thrown in the tub.

A less than glorious ending to what, for me, was such a happy visit. Fleas were part of country life and no-one panicked, though my poor Mother got near to doing so.

From North to South

The Bassetts and the Peppers were the earliest memories of dear friends for me. My Mother knew them because they were friends from my Father's childhood. She herself had come from the North-East of England – a little village south of Sunderland where her Father was head of the village school but, more importantly to him and the family, he played the organ, brilliantly. Years later we found letters from famous conductors and composers of the time, asking him to transpose orchestral works for organ and vice versa. He worked very hard, was a sweet man, rather hen-pecked by my Grandmother, especially when he sat in front of the fire in his smoking jacket. She thought it looked like a dressing gown and disapproved of his wearing it after breakfast. His family came from Scotland – Fife, where his ancestors had fled the Huguenot persecution in France and fled, as did so many "refugees" to the nearest coast of Scotland. The old house in St. Andrews remained in the family until the seventies, when the Fife branch of the last relatives domicile in Scotland, died.

My Mother also fled - to the South of England – *The Garden of England* – to get away from her Mother who, for the best possible motives, I'm pretty sure, continued to take most of my Mother's earnings from teaching. She thoroughly disapproved of her daughter – Hilda - who had a glorious and to me, unforgettable, mezzo-soprano singing voice, when her career led her in that direction and she started to be sought by choirs – anyone presenting Handel's Messiah or Mendelssohn's Elijah, to be their number one soloist and I have the sound of her part in these particularly, still in my memory, as they always will be. Granny Wright used to say it was Hilda's health that was her main concern.

This may well have been true, as Hilda had had double pneumonia in her early childhood and, of course, there was no penicillin in those days. She had also had pernicious anaemia and tired very easily, but whilst her teaching was an acceptable risk to her Mother, the musical involvement wasn't. I have a wonderful colour photograph of my Mother playing *Floradora* at the Sunderland Empire. My grandmother walked out as she thought her daughter's costume was entirely unseemly. It was a very subtly divided skirt which my Grandmother insisted was trousers. For her daughter to be singing to large numbers of people in such a rig-out, was unacceptable, so out she went. Hilda must have been pretty hurt.

Somewhere along the way my Mother had met a young man who fell in love with her, and she with him. His name, I remember, was Sydney, a much-used name in those days. He called my Mother *Celia* and his first gift to her was the score of Handel's *SAINT CECILIA*. Years later, I met him on one of my Mother's and my sorties to London – to get away from the war, she always said. (London had the odd respite.) We stayed at a homely hotel called The Coburg. It had a family atmosphere and a waitress called Edith, who really looked after us – especially me and the jars of tiddlers I kept giving her from the Round Pond! The chief pleasure for me then and a happy memory now, was playing in Kensington Gardens with children whom I later learned were Jewish escapees from Nazi Germany. We played together on the swings, slides and roundabouts. If only adults were as socially aware and functional as children. None of those I spent time with spoke a word of English. It is quite wonderful that we could play and laugh – and talk – without understanding a single spoken word. What memories did these youngsters have? One day, out with my Mother, walking near the Serpentine, I spotted the rowing boats and people on the water. My passion for being on water has always been with me but Mother was simply not strong enough to row, sensing my disappointment, she spoke to a lone young soldier sitting on a nearby seat and asked him if he would be kind enough to take us out in one of the boats. He did and we all chattered away. Again, did he make it through the War?

When we were back in the country, we heard that the Coburg had been bombed, destroyed. I asked my Mother if Edith had escaped. There are questions, she said, best not asked.

There was another lovely Jewish family with whom we became friends for the length of the stay in St. Leonards, the *posh* end of Hastings. It was a quiet and attractive place, anyway and like so many places on the South East Coast, was holding its breath in case the unmentionable happened and *they* invaded. This was far from my mind when I ran down to the beach *un-mined*, every morning with my new-found friend, the young son of the family with whom my Mother found the French language had come to the rescue while they were sipping coffee – or was it that ghastly, far-too-sweet coffee called "Camp"? We, the boy and I, ran into the sea. I couldn't swim then but he could and quite literally and without a word, taught me to swim. One morning, I imitated what he was doing and took *both* my feet off the bottom and *swam*! It was a joyous moment and so unexpected. Such a happy memory. I do hope the Family settled and thrived in this Country.

To return, briefly, to Sydney. I remember him as being tall, fair, quietly spoken and *though I might not have recognised it then, completely in love with Hilda.*

When this *avenue of pleasure* had been closed by my Grandmother, even if her motives had been of the best, Hilda had had enough. She had won a Scholarship to Oxford but actually taking it up and *going* could not be afforded, her brothers took precedence when it came to university education. Hilda had had to make do with teacher training college but loved children, so that was something she could live with. Then her singing voice had started to lead her in an exciting direction and she met the person whom I feel was the love of her life.

The trouble was, Sydney was destined to go to Kuwait to live and to work. Her Mother took Sydney aside and told him that if he took Hilda with him it would kill her, that her delicate health would not be suited to the extreme heat. But . . . *they,* Sydney and Hilda, must decide. That, of course, was that.

So, my Mother enquired and wrote letters and accepted the Headship of a Church School in a tiny village called Staple, a few miles from Canterbury in Kent. It so happened that a Mr. Pepper was Chairman of the Board of Governors. He had taken to my Mother in interview and remained her most supportive ally. Perhaps this was a modest career move but

Hilda's aim was to be independent and out of her Mother's clutches. If they fell out about it, my Mother never said. For years Granny Wright and Elizabeth, always known as "Lily", the youngest remaining daughter at home, would visit and be laden with fruit by my Father, who also would be sending boxes of fruit and vegetables by train to the North.

Will & Ann 1935

Grandpa Wright and Ann

With godparents, Susie & Tom

Will in April 1935

Granny Wright, "helping".

The bouquet after "bribe".

With a kitten friend.

With cousin Molly.

Granny Wright and Hilda, dressed for the beach.

School House

Hilda moved into School House, which was unsurprisingly next to the School. An old-fashioned iron-railing fence separated her garden from the playground. The house was a seventeenth century cottage, set back from the road and with beautiful gardens, back and front. There was a delightful rose arbour at the end of the garden path the other side from the school. I taught myself to talk in there. As I remember, this was an idyllic place.

My mother settled in to the School, joined a local choral society – I should say that the village, Wingham, some three miles away, was not regarded as *local.* Life outside any village was virtually in another country and the differences cherished. Hilda met a man who also sang in the Choir and who said he would help her with her garden. The man was *WILL,* my father-to-be.

William Percival Rye was a lovely, lovely man. On the face of it there should be no reason at all for my Mother, Hilda, to demur at the thought of being married to – and looked after by – this tall, dark and handsome fellow.

It's easy to forget the enormous part *snobbery* played in those and to a lesser extent, thank God, these days. My Mother realized she and Will did have things in common – their music, their church-going, their love of the garden and of children. The problem was, Will had had practically no education. He'd left school at fourteen and had missed much tuition through illness. He had been plagued with earache and one day heard the doctor say to his Grandmother that he, Will, would never make old bones. In the days when children were supposed to be seen and not heard, they were frequently forgotten and therefore it was often supposed that they simply didn't hear what was being said about them. Poor old love. So, he spent a lot of time battling with earache and working on the land, because that was where you worked as soon as you were able. In many ways Will was an immoveable object when it came to other people telling him what to do; an example of this was his first visit to hospital, aged eight. It had been decided, as it so often was, that he should have his adenoids and tonsils removed so was taken to Canterbury Hospital. When the op. was done, he wanted *out*, so he walked out, not really fit to do so but he followed a long procession of army vehicles, including the cooking lorry, bound for the Front. The soldiers gave him a few snacks and then forged ahead somewhat quicker than Will could walk, at his age and in his bedroom slippers.

It seemed that Will and the Army had parted company in the village of Littlebourne and somewhere near the village green next to the River Stour (pronounced *Stooer*, unlike the others in the Country!) The village policeman emerged from a little cottage off the Green and invited the boy in for a cup of tea with him and his wife. After which, having ascertained that Will had left hospital without anyone knowing, he took the boy to a door at the top of the stairs into the cellar, opened it and told him that that was where naughty boys went. Why he didn't supervise the rest of Will's journey home I can't imagine, except that everyone walked miles in those days and didn't expect to be accosted or molested, far less, raped. So Will wended his weary way back to Staple where a mild panic was going on. The hospital had sent a telegram, via the post office, to Mr. Rye – Will's Father, Henry James – and the opening of it was delayed while Mother's presence was sought because a telegram in those days of the Great War, meant only one thing; your son had been killed. Will's eldest brother, Ted, was fighting his way through France and the worst was feared. By the time they had opened the flimsy brown envelope, an exhausted child walked up the garden path. The parents were so relieved one son was not dead and another was safely home, that Will received no punishment.

So my Father grew up tall and strong, but lacking in any acedemic education and this was how the paths diverged from him and my Mother. Will had been looking after her garden, beautifully, and she appreciated this enormously. She invited him in to tea one afternoon and their conversations began, out of which they allowed their feelings to emerge. He loved her and she was fond of him.

Will didn't think for one moment that Hilda would marry him, but he felt he couldn't continue the closeness of what had become their friendship, without either going forward, or away. They discussed all the ways in which they could help each other, he with his strength and all his skills on the land, she with her learning. She would help him with his reading and his social skills. He was always polite and courteous, but actually wanted to *improve* himself, to speak without a broad rural Kent accent, to improve his violin playing and his singing; to read music better – in all these things, Hilda could be his guide and mentor and – his wife.

The only obstacles were what the *world* would say but, more importantly, what her Mother would say. The *world* kept pretty quiet, although surprised that the Headmistress of their school with a posh accent, should want to marry *Will*. Wasn't he engaged to someone else? He was - someone far more suitable and though this was true, Will spent most of his time running away from her. This had not been a happy engagement and when he broke it off to marry Hilda, she stalked each of the family in turn, including Henry, who got fed up with it and always shut himself in the garden shed if he saw her coming Hilda finally said that Will had better sort this out or their marriage was *off*. Henry eventually managed to ease or order her out of their lives, so all that remained was to persuade Mother, who had travelled down from the North with Lily, the youngest sister, to see for themselves just what was going on and whether or not this marriage should go ahead. They were persuaded, mostly, I suspect, by Will's innate kindness. The marriage took place in December, 1933.

The Old School House

In February 1935 Ann Margaret Nicholson (my Mother's insistence at the Scots connection!) Rye, was born. My happy, happy childhood started. My Mother continued teaching and I had a wonderful Nanny whom I called *Minnie.* I don't know why. My Father had rented a few acres further down the road in which he grew fruit and vegetables and kept a hundred or so chickens. They gave me great joy and some of them became pets. They would squat down as I approached and let me pick them up. I saw my first lamb being born with my Father and Henry in attendance. It was very early in the morning and the mist hadn't risen.

A word about my grandfather, Henry – he came from a long line of *Henry Jameses and James Henrys.* Later in my life, a cousin who was editor of the Hastings Observer, turned up with reams of paper and the Family genealogy which, he said, he had traced back to William the Conqueror (well whose didn't?) – who brought Hubert de *RIE* to England for a share in the spoils of war, namely, England.

Hubert had apparently hidden William in a dung-cart to save him from death in Normandy so his reward, apart from killing and the risk of being killed by Harold's horsemen, was a Baronetcy and a castle on the South Coast. I don't think our cousin said which one! The Family grew and spread itself all round the coast as far as Norfolk and all went well and prosperously until the Reformation. There were the de Ries or Ries or Ryes, enjoying life in the Court of King Henry VII until he died, when they became personae non gratae because of the breakaway from the Church engineered by Henry VIII. Catholics fled and went underground and really had a tough time for centuries.

Much land had been given to the de Ries and they became very wealthy landowners. What happened to all the land? Does the Family still own land in *RYES* a little village in Normandy? Here, of course, once the de Ries were on the run, the land became the property of Cromwell's marauding hoards and supporters.

So . . . Henry's inheritance was what had been more recently acquired in Victorian times. All the Ryes went in for large families and the land was divided by however many sons there were. Daughters only inherited when there were no sons, of course. One of these was Henry's sister, Emma, who ran the land and the farmworkers like a military operation. She was a large lady who had acquired an enormous car and could be seen bumping across the fields, driven by a frightened farmhand, to where the men were supposed to be working but apparently weren't doing so enthusiastically enough for Aunt Emma. "We shall be *ruined,*" she used to wail. "We shall be *RUINED!*" She wasn't, of course and her branch of the family acquired her land and more and more of their own. Henry's side inherited less and as one of a large family, he was entitled to even less acreage. Henry himself had sixteen children, in the middle of which was Will. They needed a regular income which small-farming wouldn't allow, so Henry had bought himself a threshing machine which he drove to all the farms in the area. Shame was brought upon the Family when Henry got his name in the local newspaper for having exceeded the speed limit, on his machine, by driving it at ten miles an hour down the main street in Faversham! I read the article years later at the same time as another piece of "scandal" presented itself in the form of a newspaper cutting, when Granny Wright was *up before the beak* and fined for not having the blackout properly in place. Thankfully, the Germans didn't spot the light from her window!

I must digress before getting on to the year of my own birth, I must recount a really sad tale of my paternal grandmother's death. The Ryes, as I have said, produced large families and as Granny Rye, aged 44, approached the birth of her sixteenth child, the midwife was called and apparently, as was her custom, packed her little midwife's bag, climbed on to her bicycle and rode to my Grandparents' cottage. She was eighty years old. The child was duly delivered and the midwife left. She left Granny Rye in agony. No-one realized what had happened – or *not* happened. The midwife had had a total aberration, as befitted her age, perhaps. She had left the afterbirth inside the mother. Granny Rye died in great pain and the rest of her family were grief-stricken. In those days, of course, you didn't *sue* people. It might have answered a lot of problems, financially, if they had done. My Father's eldest sister, Grace, took charge of the Family and my Father was her indispensable assistant. He was fifteen and felt the loss of his Mother acutely. His younger brother, Harry, became ill with grief. He developed ulcers and was told to lie in the garden with his stomach bared to the sun which, it was reckoned, would take care of it. Eventually, it did but Harry was always a bundle of nerves.

The Family, headed by her Father, Henry and Grace herself, were determined they would not be split up by other well-meaning(?) members of the wider family. . . or indeed anyone else. Their Grandmother lived up the road near the Church so she took the younger children in regularly. She was another kind soul and I remember her with affection. She and Grace, Will and my Grandfather, kept the Family together. The child who had been born as her Mother died, lived only until she was six when she became a victim of meningitis.

When I was born, the bedroom ceiling fell down. My Grandmother, a superstitious person and in attendance, of course, took that as a portent. "That child will go *far!*" she announced. She had seemed less concerned about the safety of Mother and Child as they were shielded by the nurse and the bedclothes, from falling bits of plaster. Her prediction is harder to fathom and how far is *far*?

The old School House had two staircases, one at each end of the cottage. Three bedrooms, no bathroom of course, one dining room, one drawing room and a large kitchen with outhouses; on the wall of one of them hung the tub in which we all bathed, in front of the fire. The kitchen floor was covered with home-woven mats – woven mainly by my Father – made from any piece of unwanted material – worn-out jackets, trousers or even old curtains. *In one of the television plays in which I appeared, well into the future, I was playing one of D.H. Lawrence's infamous mother-in-law characters, in his actual house and I remembered how these mats were made and was able to look fairly comfortable on camera when doing so, thanks, in large part to these early memories of my Father's mat-making all those years before.* Will had always tried to make the mats symmetrical in colour and they looked attractive. Under the mats which were most trodden upon would be the folded bed-sheets, wrapped in paper. After a week of regular depression under people's feet, the mats would *iron* the sheets, well and truly!

The first three years of life are composed of impressions. The memory of toddling down to the rose arbour and *talking* is very strong. I had convinced myself that the problem was grown-ups not understanding what you were saying, which was so very clear to *you*. I would move from that place when I heard the children playing outside the School, next door.

Watching the schoolchildren intrigued me. They all seemed so *big* but I think what struck me as odd, was that most of the little *girls* wore working boots. Then, of course, to send a child to school meant a sacrifice of their earning skills both indoors and out. There would probably be a stove to be blacked, a step to be scrubbed or chickens to be fed before these children ever got to school. How they ever learned anything is miraculous. They must have been so tired.

Church-going was *de rigueur* in our household, as in most others. We were Church of England and had a lovely old church in which to worship, sing, pray or admire hats. St. James's. had a lychgate and an avenue of Yew trees leading up to the porch. Once, when there was a family wedding, the Church was so packed that many relatives had to stand outside. Another wedding was also memorable in that photos taken of the bride and bridesmaids arriving were in brilliant sunshine but by the time she was hitched and the service was over, she and the bridegroom and other guests who *had* been able to fit into the Church walked into a snowstorm. This was in June.

One of life's childhood days was visiting the various family members on a Sunday afternoon. Sometimes I would walk, with my Father, who had made me a walking-stick, like his! We would call on his sisters – Vera and Grace in Staple and Peggy when she wasn't busy on the farm; Daisy and Nora in Wingham and Doris, who lived up the hill on the way to Heart's Delight! Mostly, the brothers, my uncles – those who weren't at war – visited us. I have realized, if I didn't fully appreciate at the time, the family love and support that there was wherever we went.

My first experience of bribery happened when I was three or four. My Mother had agreed that her daughter would present a bouquet to the person who was to open the Church Fete. I flatly refused to do so. The very thought was as embarrassing to me then as it would be now! Lady bloomin' Haywarden would have to be flowerless. My Mother then told me that was a pity because she had a new dolls' pram waiting for me if I would do this for her. I did! As a bonus – I think – I was also introduced to the then Archbishop of Canterbury, Cosmo, Lord Lang. He was very imposing in his purple cassock but seemed very pleased to meet me. I didn't know he'd been beastly to Edward VIII.

Speaking of Edward, Prince of Wales, his situation was utterly divisive. Many absolutely adored him but the rest thought him highly unsuitable for the job of being King, my parents fell into the latter faction and so, it seemed to me then, did most of their friends. He was "a n'er do well, cavorting and intending to marry *that woman*." It was the intimate association with Mrs. Simpson that riled and appalled everybody so I subsequently, still in early childhood adopted their point of view. The subject caused debates for years to come. Now I find it regrettable that it was not the Prince's involvement with Mrs. Simpson that should have alarmed people so much, but his closeness with the Nazi party in Germany. I suppose the Mrs. Simpson business elicited more *tut-tuts*. I still wonder if the friendship with Hitler and his co-horts did actually deter Adolf from invading this Country when his armies were lined up on the French coast after Dunkirk. Historians will probably disabuse me of that notion.

Meanwhile, life sailed happily along in Staple, with the visits already described, to the Bassetts, the Peppers and various relatives being regular. My Father would take me for walks in the hop gardens – oh, that wonderful smell! They don't allow anyone to walk through them now – *health and safety* I suppose. We would visit the village blacksmith where I would see, at close quarters, how an enormous Shire horse could put up with what always seemed an uncomfortable process of being shod.

In my fourth year my Mother became seriously ill and war was declared. The former had more effect on me than the latter, though I remember hearing Chamberlain's dulcet tones announcing the awful news.

The Move to Ash

When my Mother knew she had to go into hospital, she discussed my future with Will. She had been told that a kidney would have to be removed and the chances of recovery, at that time, were fifty-fifty. It was decided, unhappily for my Father, who nevertheless acquiesced, that I would go and stay with her elder sister, Susannah and her husband Tom, in Yorkshire. Suzannah had delusions of grandeur and her houses were always bigger than everyone else's. Tom was in high-level management in the railways – L.N.E.R. (London-North-Eastern-Railway) but even at my tender age I could see how he was bossed about when he was at home. During a visit on another occasion, Uncle Tom asked if I would like to go out in a boat on the lake in their local park. That was an exciting prospect. The trouble was, as Tom got himself and me into the boat, it drifted away from its little wooden pier and Suzannah fell in the water. Later, the family would laugh at the tale, but at the time she was livid and walked off and left us to it. We returned to dry land and followed her, at a cracking pace. Her fur coat was soaked. She shouted at Tom and he said quietly to me: "You see, Ann, what I have to put up with." I was somehow touched that he had confided in me. It brought about a closeness between us and I loved him.

The visits, though, were mostly enjoyable and I learned the Yorkshire accent from Michael, next door and to love the cinema with Suzannah.

My Mother, thankfully for all of us, recovered slowly from what was a major operation – the scar went from the middle of the back and down the left side of the tummy. I was aghast when I was shown it. Hilda would tell the tale of how the first meal that was offered her in hospital when she started to recover, was steak and kidney pie. Hmmm.

Doctor Fraser was our regular – and costly – G.P. as the National Health Service had not yet arrived. When the N.H.S. did arrive, post-war, we found it difficult to forgive Fraser for telling my Mother that he wasn't paid to answer questions on tuppence a week. That, after all the money he had received from us because of my Mother's ill health! He told my Father that the old School House was too damp for Hilda and that he should seriously think about moving to the next, bigger village, Ash, and into a more modern house. What became known as *the phoney war* was a bit eerie but life went on and Will found a larger, slightly more modern house to rent in Ash, "St. Peter's", but Hilda would have to continue teaching in Staple and Will working the land there.

The day we moved was memorable for me as our cat, Pongo, had to travel in the car with us. Great excitement. Pongo had been rescued by My Mother when he was a year old and I was besotted with him and he with me, I think, despite the fact that in photographs I realize I used to hold him round his top half with his legs dangling. He put up with absolutely anything from me.

We had a small and rather adorable little Austin Seven in which – and briefly in the back seat on my own - I had once crawled into the passenger seat from the back of the car, released the handbrake and slipped rather rapidly down the hill. I was still three years old! Pandemonium broke out but I think the relief my parents felt overcame any undue recriminations. That little car was building up experiences – my Father had driven it through the back of the barn in which it was housed. It lasted us a long time, though.

Things did then!

So we moved into St. Peter's, in the village of Ash. My Mother was asked to become Head of the Kelsey (Church) School and my Father acquired orchards and open ground – including a partridge run – behind St. Peter's. All the houses on the village street, backed on to my Father's land and we subsequently became friendly with all the people who would walk down their cottage garden paths and talk to us. They all seemed to be lovely, kind people – mostly women of *a certain age,* whose husbands had fought in the first World War and who were now widowed and on their own. Mr. and Mrs Blakelock were in the first of the row. He had been in the Royal Navy in the Great War and one day when I was a little older, he gave me the hammock he had used on board. I immediately got my Father to fix it up between two branches of a tree and I would luxuriate, become a sailor on the high seas who chewed apples and read Enid Blyton. I had that hammock for years.

Further up the road was Ruby Sparkman, who became a special friend and looked after my pet hen when, as a touring actor, I had to be away working; next door to her Miss Burton, who had a sister who lived at the end of the village and whose front room was their place of business – i.e. sewing, repairing, altering and making dresses of all shapes and sizes. They too, would have been at home in Cranford. Then Miss Inge, who looked after her Father who was blind. Mrs Russell was, I think, the last of the really chatty cottage owners and she had endless trouble with her daughter and her escapades with *men*. I listened avidly.

So here we were, happily ensconced. The Church was now St. Nicholas and it was at the highest point of the village. This became very significant when the war started in earnest.

In the middle of the village, on the left, was the baker's shop owned and run by Mrs. Errington. Without fail, when the milkman and his horse got to our house, the horse would take himself and cart down to Mrs. Errington. I'm sure bread isn't good for horses, but he seemed to like it and he lived for a long time. The milkman got used to walking down the street to persuade him to resume the milk round. Milk was delivered out of churns; you took your jug to the door and Mr. Homersham, the milkman, would dole out the required amount with a ladle, from his churn.

Opposite the bakery was Bickers' confectionary. Cigarette and newspaper shop. Mrs. Bicker ran her own shop and nobody got the wrong side of her. If your paper wasn't delivered, it certainly wasn't *her* fault. I remember several arguments about this between her and my Mother. I doubt if she, my Mother, won. Both my parents smoked cigarettes. She preferred du Maurier and later on, Craven A and she used very carefully to detach the cork-like paper stuck on to the end of the cigarette and smoke it like one of an untipped variety. When I was a little older and could go to the shop by myself, I would give Mrs. Bicker half-a-crown for a packet of Mother's Craven-A and there would be twopence change, with which I was allowed to buy an ice cream. "Penny Cornets" were the thing then. Wafer-filled ice cream was called "a wafer" and I think it was a little more expensive – twopence perhaps?

Vye's the grocer's shop was opposite the Baker's on the other side of Chequer Lane and on the corner of the main village street. Mr. Jenner was in charge there and once a week, holding my Mother's hand, we would walk down to order the week's groceries. Mr. Jenner would fetch each item that was asked for and put it on the counter, he and Mother chatting the while. We would leave and the groceries would be packed into boxes and delivered in a Vye's van, later.

All this and these people may seem like *too much information*. They are not intended to be minutely imprinted on the memory as they are on mine, but to give the background of where we lived and how we lived. Individual shops owned and run by people whom everyone knew. When you walked down the Street – that was what it was, perhaps unimaginatively called – these were the places and people you passed, all the way up to the Church. I'll leave them there while I return to the wider world, of which I was largely unaware when we first moved. I do remember being excited by the *3* and the *9* of 1939 turning into the big 4 0. What a year that was to be, when the war began in earnest. Fighters overhead and bombs and bombers. I can still block my ears with my fists at night and hear the loud engines of the Junkers and the thuds as excess bombs were unloaded before the return to Northern France.

Britain On Her Own

So, a reality check must be recorded. My backcloth behind the world and the Nation's on-stage drama which was becoming more and more of a tragedy.

> *In London, two million 19 – 27 year-olds are called up; The Thames is frozen for the first time since 1888 and the worst storm for a century is recorded. In France the Germans are gaining more and more advances North of Paris; In Berlin The Nazis warn that listening to foreign radio is punishable by death.*

It was many years later, when I was married to Andrew, that I was told about the plight of the Scandinavian countries at that time because of the machinations, betrayals and invasions by both Russians and Germans. Mind you, I gather Norwegian fishermen weren't too pleased at having the British sinking mines off their coast as a deterrent to invading German ships. As the enemy took over, Andrew had been amongst the last contingent of British troops to be rescued by our brave ships as they waited off the coast at

Narvik for little Norwegian fishing boats to take them off the shore and towards the waiting ship. Many didn't make it, but Andrew did. All that was imparted to me some fifty years after the event.

Here is an excerpt from Nora's husband, Uncle Albert Pettman's journals, relevant to these times:-

We have had 5 hours in port and are sailing for Norway. It's bitterly cold and far too rough for mine-laying. Hope the weather is better in the Fjords. Everyone's nerves are being strained to the utmost. No sleep for nights and work, work, work (laying mines in waters under Enemy control.) It's a job that must be done, though who can come off watch for two <u>hours' sleep with large "pills" (mines) all around you.</u>

<u>Later</u>: After a few days' leave, we sailed full speed for Norway, Bergen again, loaded with 266 mines which we layed successfully. Back to base and loaded up with 260 special submarine mines . . .

HMS Manxman

On our way up to Granny Wright in Durham, bearing fruit and veges, I remember vividly the troops that were crowded on to the train. Sailors with famous ships' names on their caps. As so often, I wonder where they were going and if they got back. Albert did but Manxman didn't escape torpedos later on. My Mother had a worried look that I had started to notice but sometimes thought it was because I'd been naughty. (I was a little daredevil and called myself John.) Maybe she had reason for concern!

I do remember well the enthronement of the Dalai Lama because he was the same age as I was and therefore very grown-up. It was my first awareness of being protective of someone I admired and, yes, loved.

> *Chamberlain and Churchill "jaw-jawing" with the Supreme Allied War Council; Czech Jews are ordered to cease any economic activity; H.M.S. DARING is sunk; the liner, Queen Elizabeth is sent, secretly, to the U.S. for the duration of the war; Royal Canadian Airforce personnel arrive in Britain.*

What a debt we owed to those Canadians – in all areas of war.

War In Earnest

On my own home front, I had become friendly with Michael. I suppose he was my first leading man, though he was shorter and less robust than me. I was his *older woman* as my birthday was six months before his. We had an obsession with home-making which later on worried my Mother. She kept finding us in bed together in our new little house, wherever it was. Michael was good at making things – his father, Percy, was a masterbuilder with his own business – so there was never a shortage of material. We vowed we wouldn't tell anyone where we lived and this was very nearly our undoing. *We* had built a little nest inside the shed where all the prepared wood was kept. We made ourselves a delightful home under a pile of planks which rested on trestles, thus leaving a gap between them and the wooden floor. We had the usual table, chair and bed, with pretend cups of tea and, if we were fortunate, a biscuit or two. Our lighting came from two candles. Percy, having come to inspect his timbers, saw a little light from under the pile of planks and was not only baffled, but perplexed. All was revealed as he had the men move all the wood – including, of course, the *roof* of our house. There we were, caught in the act of tea and biscuits by candlelight! Percy completely lost it. Candles were hastily snuffed out and we were forbidden ever to enter the wood store again. I think it was some time before Michael and I understood the implications of candles, wood and enclosed spaces. Well, it was good while it lasted. We subsequently erected tents in the orchards. Still *secret* of course, but somehow always discovered by my Mother. I can't believe that she thought I was in danger of being pregnant at such an early age, but she just didn't like Michael and me in bed together!

As we grew a little older, we discovered more things we could do together, have tricycle races which were great fun to start with then Michael, as was his wont, I'm afraid, got fed up with being beaten, opted out of the race and waited for me as I circled the fish pond and pushed me and tricycle into the mucky pond. I, on the other hand, had stopped halfway in the middle of a running race at the annual Church Fete, and waited for Michael to catch up. Back to the ungentlemanly pond incident. I splashed about a bit; his Mother arrived and then fetched my Grandmother, who happened to be staying while my Mother was teaching. Granny Wright was pretty formidable, grabbed my hand and let rip at Michael and his Mother, then took me home where she removed all my clothing, tut-tutting at all the weeds and slime that had clung to me and put me in the bath. When you *are* a grandparent you become the *most* protective, *most* responsible and *most* loving person on earth. Granny Wright had brought up her own children very strictly, but she indulged me in all things, even when I used her sharp scissors to cut her net curtains from top to bottom, following the patterns. Still with scissors in hand, I gather, I cut my hair. It was Mother, not Grandmother, who was very cross!

The fish-pond incident with Michael was not referred to again, by any of us and Michael strove hard to be helpful to me in every way. I had been given a dolls' house, made by Mr. Hyde, the Staple village carpenter, from a table that my parents no longer wanted. It was a majestic mansion – Michael thought so too and built me furniture for all the rooms. Very impressive. From then on our *moving in together* was a vicarious experience in my beautiful dolls' house. Alas, our uninterrupted bliss was almost at an end when I saw Michael peeing in the coal scuttle in the drawing room of his house. His Mother was in the kitchen. I must say, though surprised, I was terribly impressed at the way he aimed and . . . fired, as it were, straight into the scuttle. He told me I could do it, too. I wasn't sure how to go about it and from that moment discovered the anatomical differences between us. I just couldn't *aim* in the efficient way Michael had, so I, the carpet – and Michael – ended up, well, saturated. Inevitably, Michael's Mother, Mabel, returned from the kitchen to see what we were up to. My Mother was called this time. Words were few and I was taken home very firmly by the hand, sodden clothes removed and plonked into the bath again. What a learning curve!

German Blitzkrieg

German blitzkrieg in Western Europe; British Government bans all strikes; German Armies 35 miles from Paris; French government moves south to Tours. Brigadier-General Charles de Gaulle is appointed Under Secretary for War; Italy declares war on France and Britain; In London the biggest air raid shelter is opened, eventually intended to house 11,000.

So, Britain was on her own and Churchill gave his *finest hour* speech which I do believe I heard, with my parents. Their terrible anxiety was never passed on to me, though I had started to pray – *God, please let the war be over and can I have a little black dog.* I prayed that every night for the duration of the war. The war ended first and the little black dog came later. Now, however, awful things were going on and I did listen to the news at 9.00 every night with my parents. They and most thinking people, were expecting the last stages of this dreadful war would be fought on British soil. No wonder my Mother – all mothers – had worried faces. All the little fishing boats were gone. We saw them every week when we went to buy our freshly-caught fish straight from the sea into the boats, then our shopping basket and the back seat of the car. The boats, including our favourite – *JUDY* - had gone to Dunkirk.

> *Many boats were sunk in the region of the pier and further out to sea, another "defence" presumably. Immediately after the war was over the fisherman we had been friends with, would be rowing people round on a sight-seeing tour of the wrecks.*

The Luftwaffe had been attacking British convoys in the Channel so things were definitely hotting up. However, still uninvaded, Village life carried on with great adventures in the fields and orchards, shared now by two of Mrs. Errington – the baker's - nephews, who were now regularly sent away from London to our village and I adored them, followed them everywhere and got into more trouble, though less *personal,* than I ever did with Michael.

My Father joined the Home Guard. My Mother used to

say "Heaven help the Country if it depends on your Father to keep the enemy at bay!" She was right, actually, apart from cleaning his rifle every Sunday morning, my Father was as likely to *use* it as he was to join the German Army. One afternoon, as we drove to see his sisters, Doris, Daisy and Nora in the next village, he stopped the car and handed my Mother a telegram. She opened and read it to herself, then handed it to Will. He would not be called up as he was in a *reserved occupation,* a job essential to the Nation – i.e. feeding it. They hugged each other with relief and the Home Guard was given the privilege of his presence. Every Sunday after Church, with a clean rifle, he would go and join his mates and crawl along ditches and behind hedgerows, pretending to be snakes and hissing at unsuspecting walkers as they passed near to them. Boys were ever boys.

Church on Sunday was de rigueur and we always went to Matins at 11.00 a.m. I can remember every person in the St. Nicholas's choir now. Minnie Smallman who sang sharp – even I could tell that; Wilfred Goldup; Rachel Goldup; Walter Smith; MR. Webberley and John Foat of whom, more anon. He was the village butcher and landowner with a very disagreeable wife. Why? Later!

Because of my Father's job of *feeding the Nation* we were still able to run the car – the little green Austin Seven I *drove* down the hill from our house in Staple. We had petrol coupons – I think they were called "E" coupons and the E for Emergency petrol was a red colour so that, on inspection, it could be seen to be *legal* and no questions were asked. Woe betide anyone who had *illegally* acquired red petrol. We were able to pop down to the sea which I always loved to do, but our beach at Sandwich was mined and barbed-wired. A mile further east, towards Ramsgate, there was a long breeze-block wall from the top of which angle-iron posts protruded and looked (did they?) from the sea as though they were guns pointing at any intruder. They fooled me, anyway, until I was disabused but I still thought they might be a deterrent. Doubt if the Germans would have been so gullible.

Speaking of the road to Ramsgate, there were one or two important buildings – Pfeizers for one and one of the firework makers but what makes that part of the country memorable for me is the building in which C.E.M.A. (a branch of E.N.S.A) concerts would be held. I remember seeing Coco the Clown, very famous in his time but as we were enjoying a cup of tea at the interval, an Army Officer approached us, looked at me but spoke to my Mother. I don't remember his exact words, but what he was saying was that all the little children were to be evacuated from this vulnerable area, so close to the French coast, so how would her little girl feel about going away to safety with lots of other little children. I was neither deaf nor daft. I had no intention of going anywhere without my parents. I clung to my Mother and she, hesitating for just a moment, looked at the officer and said: "I think whatever the threat, we would rather stay together." He argued the toss a bit then left. The thought of leaving my beloved parents, the village, friends and animal friends, appalled me. My whole world was under threat in those few moments.

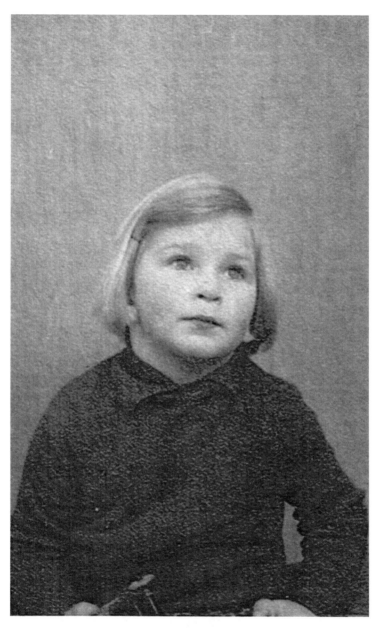

Ann's first portrait.

Ida Harden, dear friend.

Peter Harden with Ann.

Uncle Bill and family.

Always eat alone!

With beloved Pongo.

Will in Home Guard uniform.

Hilda in the latest fashion.

The Luftwaffe And Us

Up in the skies the battles had begun. The Luftwaffe had started bombing our airfields and on the other side of the Channel, we had been bombing theirs, to stop them bombing ours, which rather took the enemy by surprise, I think. History in-the-making was our reality now. I began to listen to the News as avidly as my parents and imagined I knew the Readers. I used to go to the back of the large radio set, look through one of the slits, see the red light and there would be Stuart Hibbert, reading the news. Years and years later, as I stood waiting for red lights in radio studios, I remembered vividly, peering into the back of that old wireless. John Snagge, who later commentated on many a Boat Race; Frank Phillips, very strong-voiced and Alvar Lidell, with whom I did a radio play in the sixties – he was playing . . . a newsreader, himself.

Our village – Ash – had a very deep-voiced siren. I didn't think it was a *proper* siren because everywhere else, particularly London, had a wailing sound, ours was a moaning sound. Nevertheless, it worked and people hurried to air raid shelters. We didn't. My Mother was convinced that we could be shot at twenty times before we ever reached the shelter. Poor Will, by law he had had, with some help from one of the farm hands, to dig out shelters all over what was called the *estate*. I remember "helping" him when I was four and getting a terrible nose-bleed whilst I was in the base of the shelter and running in to Eva, our lovely maid who also kept an eye on me when my Mother was teaching. I think the association of sheltering from bombs and my own blood were a bit much. Anyway, we never used any of the shelters. Hilda told people that whenever she saw pictures taken after London bombings, the one part of a house that would be left standing was the stairs. So that's where we went – under the stairs – until Moaning Minnie told us it was safe to emerge.

> *In mid-August of 1940 the Lutwfaffe starts targeting Southern England; Trotsky is assassinated with an ice-pick; Churchill makes an historic speech about "the few" – our amazing young airforcemen – and "never in the field of human conflict has so much been owed by so many to so few."*

Now I wonder if I do actually remember Churchill saying these things, but what was life-changing was the Battle of Britain in the skies above us which continued well into September. We would go to the garden beyond the orchard my Father had given over to my Mother from which we had a treeless view of the dog-fights, as they were called, going on over our heads. Were we foolhardy? Perhaps we were, but I think what was happening seemed remote, as though we were protected by the space above and between us and them. *Them* being all the protagonists, ours and theirs. The Spitfire, now an iconic piece of war machinery, had the speed to outfly the Messerschmidt most of the time, but the Germans knocked out a lot of them and one of the haunting, upsetting memories still is of a pilot baling out, but being shot to pieces whilst doing so. Many jumped with their parachutes in flames. Ours and theirs. One Spitfire crashed just across the field and Farmer Benbow's meadow. I don't know how soon we dared to do so, but we, the Field boys, with me tagging along, ran all the way to the little copse into which a crashed Spitfire had landed and while the boys were collecting fallen-off bits, I was small enough still to climb, unnoticed, into the cockpit. I still maintain that the seat was still warm from the human body that inhabited the plane until so recently. Men in uniform were ever on the look-out – and the hunt – for children and grown-ups who dashed to the site of crashed aircraft. Either they had already done their inspection, or they were in hot pursuit of us, I now don't remember. In any case, it was risky and again, probably foolhardy. It's what you did. We had a big drawer in the mahogany chest in the hall, full of schrapnel. The spoils of our war. What we had not known at the time was that a Messerschmidt had crashed near the recreation ground – the "*rec*"- and the villagers who lived nearby had run towards the plane and apparently rescued the pilot who, by all reliable accounts, had welcomed his capture by these kind people!

There were unfortunate spin-offs while the battle above was raging. Joyce Carnell, the garage proprietor's daughter, was hurrying down the village street to get home and a "rogue" German fighter plane, presumably on his way home across the Channel, decided to release his remaining bullets in her direction and killed her. The thing is, our Parish Church, as I have described, was on top of a hill and being only three miles in from the coast, was the first important landmark for the incoming planes and the village street guided them to Canterbury and on to London.

In addition to the enemy's knowledge of the whereabouts of the village Church, was its knowledge of a place called Durlock, a hamlet between Ash and Staple within sight of Vera's bungalow. Durlock was the site of an enormous military camp for the Royal Artillery and *we knew that They knew* because Lord Haw-Haw, the now infamous spy, described it on the radio – I heard him. Durlock was amazingly well camouflaged, surrounded by orchards, but it had been spotted and shouted about on *our wireless.* Perhaps as a result of this leakage, the soldiers were spread out into homes in the village and we had Arthur and Eddie billeted on us. My Mother had a memorable up-and-downer with the C.O. whose name was Major Drake Brockman. I can see him now, standing at the front door telling my Mother that palliasses would be delivered to go into the large front bedroom as there was only a double-bed in there. My Mother absolutely refused to have the bedroom carpet *littered with straw* and said what on earth was wrong with the men sharing . . . a large bed. Well, in those days any risks were simply not an issue – except with the Major, but he was obviously reluctant to explain what was the meaning of homosexuality to a rather formidable female opponent who wouldn't have known what he was talking about. He gave up and the boys shared the bed with, as far as we knew, no shenanigans.

Eddie had a lovely, smiling face and obviously loved children. He was kind and always seemed to be laughing. Arthur was more serious, possibly officer material. Our house became like theatrical digs. They went off to *rehearse* their manoeuvres in the daytime and came home to eat with us at night. They weren't with us for long, six months perhaps, before they were sent off to war. I kept asking my parents where they had gone, but was told we would never know – *Careless Talk Costs Lives* – everything was very secret – except from Lord Haw-Haw apparently. Only recently, I looked at the gravestones in the British and Commonwealth Cemetery at Bayeux to see if by any chance *our* soldiers names were on any of them. The average age was about twenty-five and there are four thousand young men interred there.

The Hardens, Max And Heinz

Next door to Bickers, the newspaper and confectionary shop and opposite the Chemist, was a large, sprawling shop called *HARDENS*. It was on two floors and sold clothes, ladies and gents, shoes, ladies and gents, lingerie, haberdashery and anything else that you could either doff or blow your nose on.

My Mother and I spent many hours in Hardens' shop, not only shopping, but not being able to escape from Ida Harden who just couldn't bear not to make a sale and Mother, uncharacteristically, was a soft touch.

The black sign of "Utility" on a white label was now attached to most articles of clothing and, not to put too fine a point on it, the quality of those goods was not always of the best. All part of the Nation's wartime economy drive.

Of course, we were no longer able to import anything. All merchant shipping, especially from the United States, was having an appalling time. We heard the reports on the Wireless.

So, shopping sprees at Hardens on a regular basis were the order of most months. My Father went through a lot of boots and wellies, jerkins and jackets. I was growing out of clothes rapidly and Ida, later to be known as "Aunty Ida", just loved sorting out my wardrobe needs – all economy labelled stuff – not always to my Mother's taste, but then none of the items lasted long! The "liberty bodice" was a must. We all, particularly children, had to be wrapped up against the cold – "keep your kidneys warm" we were told, especially, I suppose, by my Mother, who had only one kidney to cosset now.

"Uncle" Bertie Harden was a person to love and we all did. He had First World War injuries (as did so many older friends), walked with a limp and arthritis had set in and gave him much pain. He also had a finger which he used to try and get me to straighten, to no avail. It was unmoveable. He and Mr. Gooding, who sang in the Church choir, as already mentioned, had worked for the Hardens all his life; both he and Bertie wore tape measures round their necks and were usually to be found in that part of the shop that was for the *gents*. The ladies entered up a flight of worn-down stone steps at the front of the building.

Ida could be irritating, especially when she got into the hard-selling mode, but after a time, she and Mother became friends – I think Ida appreciated our support and we her faithful attention, even if it could be a bit overwhelming at times. We all, My Father, Uncle Bertie and I felt great affection for each other and as time went on, visited each others' houses. Tea at our house was rather more generous than tea at theirs which became a family joke. Ida would always very carefully count the buns! Their son, John, was in "Intelligence" as it was called. The Intelligence Corps was what it was and Ida tended to remind people fairly regularly of this. He fetched up in Germany and brought all sorts of Nazi memorabilia – flags and badges, back with him.

One of Ida's finer moments was when she chose to put up German Jewish soldiers who had miraculously escaped the Nazis and were now attached to the British Army at Durlock, the camp near Staple. My Mother joined forces with her and we received Heinz Harpuder into our life and our home.

Max, another in similar circumstances, stayed with the Hardens. These men, the victims of persecution and threats of death camps in their own Country, whose families were tragically left behind and suffering, had risked death by escaping to our Country and joining an Army which might help to save their Country from the horrors of Nazism. They were both musicians. Heinz a beautiful pianist and Max a gifted violinist. How on earth did they cope with being *soldiers*?

The time these two soldiers spent with us was, in my childhood memory, an absolute joy. My Mother, as I have said before, had a divine mezzo-soprano singing voice; my Father played the violin (with the Raggle Taggle Gypsies) but Max *really* played the violin and Heinz was an amazing and sensitive pianist. He taught me a lot when I later used to accompany Mother. I must have been a very poor substitute!

I daresay it was a great relief for them, coming home each day from tough army duties, to a home-cooked meal followed by the *music-making* which must have given them the joy that only playing music with like-minded people, can.

Heinz and my Mother became great friends. Later in life I wondered if they were in love. They would spend hours talking and Heinz would tell my Mother what he could from news that was leaked out of Germany. For example, I learned from eavesdropping that his Mother was trying to live on sawdust. There was no food, particularly for a Jew in hiding. This played on my young mind and when we went to Mr. Foat, the butcher, the sawdust on his floor suddenly conveyed a whole new and sinister meaning. So this was what Heinz's Mother was living on? Such things are not to be dwelt upon but war has unsuspected side-effects, particularly on children. I think that subsequently all the family that Heinz left behind ended their lives in concentration camps.

There are other happenings which I now wonder if I heard during one of My Mother's conversations with Heinz. The plot to kill Hitler was one of them, but what I remembered most was the *stringing up* of the failed assassins with piano-wire and, hideous as it seems to me now, led to my giving my toys the same treatment on the bars of the piano stool. I don't know what I answered when Mother asked me what I thought I was doing but I do wonder if she realized I must have heard about this from *somewhere*. Such things are not to be dwelt upon but again, war has unsuspected side-effects, on children.

The blackout had its own horrors for me as I simply hated going to sleep in the dark. It seemed – and still seems to me - a totally claustrophobic experience. In wartime, of course, it was difficult to throw light on anything to solve this problem so my bedroom door had to be open at all times and I daresay when it was assumed I had dropped off I was, in fact, listening to everything that I could hear. Perhaps I was a natural for a life in the *theatre* as I was wide awake till dawn on many an occasion. The other advantage of being awake was that when my Mother came to my room, she would shut the door and open the blackout on to the night sky and tell me about the stars. The sound of our bombers on their way across the Channel would penetrate anyone's consciousness and so we would be pressed against the window, she and I, counting the planes as they flew, quite low, above us.

Later, of course, Mother would come into my room as the drone of the aircraft could be heard again. We would count those returning and although it was almost a game to me, my Mother would make sure I could do enough sums to answer *how many didn't come back?*

Coventry Bombed And Chamberlain Dies

Coventry devastated by the worst air raid of the war; Liverpool bombed by an intensive air raid and Southampton suffers severe damage from Luftwaffe bombs;

Neville Chamberlain dies of cancer, aged 71; controversy still continues over his Munich agreement with Hitler. Chaplin's long-awaited film, The Great Dictator, withering political satire, arrives too late for blitz-torn London. Britain engaged in fighting in North Africa, taking Tobruk airport. 100,000 Italian troops captured and British are bombing Italian cities. Tobruk captured by British troops. BBC lifts its ban on conscientious objectors . . .

. . . which brings me to Mabel Armstrong's (Michael's mother) house guest, Miss Cochrane. Mabel's sister, Audrey, frightfully well off, lived in Bromley and every now and then would send a friend or relative to the *safety* of Ash. Miss

Cochrane had been bombed out and came to live with the Armstrongs. Her nephew, John, was a conscientious objector. He used to come and visit, almost in a cloak and dagger fashion. Very few people were sympathetic to these young men who were often convinced that the stand they were taking was for the most moral of reasons – they could not contemplate killing anyone. Of course, there were those who couldn't contemplate *being killed* but on the whole they were weeded out and imprisoned. John had been released from prison and was doing some kind of war work which meant he was *acceptable.* To my parents' credit, no uncompromising point of view was ever expressed and while continuing regularly to have tea with Michael, I chattered away to John – and it never occurred to me to question who or what he was. Between him and Miss Cochrane there was great affection.

In the first two and a half years of war, we and our wonderful Commonwealth friends, seemed to be fighting in so many theatres of war. I think the news that we heard nightly probably encouraged positive thinking. Mind you, when London had its worst bombing and the whole area round St. Paul's was devastated, we did wonder – where next? Perhaps divine intervention had kept the Cathedral itself miraculously free from the rain of high explosives. We heard about the sinking of H.M.S. Hood and the German invasion of Russia. I think perhaps the worried look, almost always on my Mother's face, may have eased a little as Hitler's armies, lined up across the Channel, twenty-one miles from us, were gradually removing and being sent to the Russian Front. Neither we nor they knew of the horrors they were to face, whether German or Russian.

I used to follow my Father round during the daytimes and *help* him with a myriad of jobs in the orchards, the open plantations where the tomatoes grew and the back-breaking jobs of planting potatoes, gathering rhubarb or picking strawberries. The most difficult to dig up was horseradish. There was some demand for it but if only the return had reflected the really hard job of harvesting it. It was as tough as a pair of Will's old boots. I used the word *help* advisedly. I think I got in his way a lot of the time, but the people who worked for him were always nice to me and I enjoyed my *out*side world. Will worked incredibly hard. Fruit, vegetables and flowers had to be ready twice a week for the lorry to take them in their bushel and half-bushel boxes to Covent Garden. The flowers were a joy to me. Daffodils, Narcissi and Tulips grew, in that order, in profusion all over the floor of the orchards and down the sides of the long grass paths between. If there had been rain, the long stems and leaves would go up your sleeves and make your arms wet when you were gathering them. Didn't like that bit. He was a great *digger*, Will. He was so rhythmical when using the spade and I really think he preferred it to the tractor. Before Winter came he would have several acres dug up in neat, symmetrical rows. He used a scythe in the same rhythmical fashion. When the long grass got out of hand, I can see him now, swinging the scythe through the thick grass at the foot of the River Plum trees. They were the best flavoured plums ever – what happened to them, I wonder. Anyway, there he'd be, cutting back the grass and sometimes there would be very agitated clucking sounds. Not our chickens, but wild partridges who would nest in the long grass and I would beseech my Father not to cut their heads off with the scythe. He didn't – they heard him coming and were ready for a rapid, if panicky departure. Originally, I daresay, they came from a partridge run we had inherited near to one of the old boundary hedges. It had been dismantled not long after we moved to Ash and I like to think that the birds were let out and therefore avoided an unceremonious death. Incredibly satisfying work, even if you were just being a *nuisance* as I was frequently but affectionately called.

In the evenings I would go down the Street and call on the Lamings, who lived in a little row of cottages before you got to Bickers' shop. They were called Alice and Annie. One had been a teacher – Alice – and I think Annie had looked after their Mother, as one daughter would, in those days. Alice had been to see my Mother for advice about her pension and, yet again, I listened to the conversation in which Alice said she was simply not getting what she should have been getting. My Mother had taken on the job of Treasurer for twenty amalgamated charities, chaired by the Bishop of Dover. A brief but comedy moment comes to mind. All the Trust members were assembled in our drawing room, the Bishop at the head of the table. The door obviously wasn't properly closed and our dear cat entered, with the straps of a petticoat in his mouth – he just couldn't resist pulling things from where they hung in the airing cupboard. He dragged the whole garment in and dumped it in front of the Bishop. He was a lovely man and neither panicked nor reprimanded while my Mother calmly picked the petticoat up, then came back for our feline intruder, who had settled down for the meeting. He did that sort of thing and just *adored* coffee (in a saucer, of course) and biscuits. On this occasion he was not invited to that part of the meeting and business was resumed. When my Mother broached the problems Alice Laming was having, everyone must have assumed that Alice was looking for some charitable gesture, at which Alice had later shouted: "I want my *rights* not charity!" I made myself scarce. This loss of cool by Alice really upset me. What were her *rights* and why couldn't my Mother help? I'm pretty sure, with the Welfare State in its infancy, her *rights* would be few. I do believe my Mother was able to sort something out. She was always good like that. When her pupils became young adults she continued to battle for them, especially the girls, to enable them to have the same chances as their male counterparts and get to university.

Back to the sisters Laming. I had been allowed, perhaps encouraged, to call on them every evening after tea and was always given a kind welcome. They would sit me down at their dining table, always covered with a Chenille tablecloth, and say: "Would you like a game?" knowing full well that was *really* why I had come. The oil lamp on the table would be turned up. Many people didn't have electricity in those days. We used to play Snap and Beg o' My Neighbour and *Muggins;* this had to be played *after* a game of Snap when you had got so used to yelling *SNAP* when your cards and your opponent's were identical that you were not at all prepared for the opposite reaction which was total silence and if anyone broke it they were called "Muggins" in a suitably derisory fashion. We played draughts and Ludo and other now long-forgotten board games – "Halma" and "Sorry" (what on earth were they about!) I think I had grown out of Snakes and Ladders. When we weren't playing games we were doing jig-saw puzzles and I loved every minute of my time spent with them. Ten years further on it broke my heart when Alice died in the workhouse hospital in Canterbury, one of many elderly patients in a long line of beds. What had this bright former headmistress, with such a kind heart, come to? Perhaps if she'd had *rights* that were a fairer reflection of her hard work teaching, she would not have *come to this.*

Granny Wright popped in and out of our lives. It was a long journey from the North East but when my Father couldn't leave things in the growing season and if my Mother, comparatively soon after a major operation, couldn't cope with carrying cases, Granny Wright would come to us and there are numerous snaps of her sitting in a garden full of flowers, amongst the apple blossom and a most incongruous juxtaposition comes to mind, of Granny in a deck chair on the beach, with her black clothes and elaborate black hat, always held in place with a long and decorative hatpin. (My son James, now in his forties, took a fancy to this and has it pinned to his kitchen wall!)

Granny was very good to me and we used to wander round the village together, hand in hand and almost always end up at the Church. Granny's family had been Catholics and she had transferred her loyalties to the Church of England when she married my Grandfather whose family, in turn, had transferred their allegiance from the Presbyterian church in Scottish days, to the English Church. This, I think, was quite bold in those days, but my Grandfather, who was a profoundly gifted musician, became the leading light in his Church's musical life. He played the organ magnificently and had acquired the reputation of being able to transpose any orchestral work for organ and vice-versa. Long after his death my Son and I found those letters from conductors of the day, which had asked him to transpose organ works for their orchestras to play and from other organists to reverse the arrangement for them. He also taught, smoked a pipe and still wore his smoking jacket for as much of the morning as my Grandmother would allow. Poor old boy, she did boss him about. At night, when my Mother and I were staying, he and she would alternate their pre-slumber room-to-room exchanges between crosswords and algebraic problems!

They were very close and when he died, just before the war, she had felt his death very keenly.

Back to Granny in Ash. In the Church she would inspect all the names on the flagstones very thoroughly, tell me not to touch the Virgin Mary's picture – she obviously hadn't quite cast off the Catholic respect for the Holy Mother, especially when a child's grubby hands might sully the Virgin's face. Then we would wander round the churchyard where the sheep would graze because there was a shortage of manpower to keep the grass cut. Granny would study the gravestones as closely outside as she had inside the church and I would follow suit. I remember vividly coming across a gravestone that I found very upsetting because it was for a child of four. I said to Granny – "How sad. Just as she was getting to know the world." As a five-year old I, of course, already had this advanced knowledge. Nevertheless, I really meant what I said and I could almost certainly find the grave now. It was on one of these occasions of our ramblings that we came across the graves of the Germans, *outside* the graveyard, with unnamed crosses. Even then, that seemed a little unfair to me, but then I wasn't being shot down by them. Unlike Joyce Carnell, of course.

The Rights Of Jews In France

Petain imposes further restrictions on the rights of Jews; German troop movements on the Russian border; 12,000 Jews arrested under Petain's orders, for "plotting to hinder Franco-German co-operation."; the Bismarck is sunk; Germany and Italy expel the U.S. Consuls. "Blithe Spirit" by Noel Coward opens in London.

A word about this last item. It is a serious work in the guise of farce. Rather like the film *A Matter of Life and Death* it was a kind of optimistic reassurance that this life might not be *it*. Coward's "war effort" it might be said. It was . . . supposed to amuse but at the same time to help, perhaps, those who had lost a beloved husband, father or son.

We children became somewhat obsessed with *spies*. We saw them all over the place. One such was a burly chap with a stick and a cloth cap, who used to hang about on the corner of Vye's, the grocer's shop garage. The old Vye van came and went but this man didn't. He always seemed to be there and we would stare at him, rather rudely, I suppose, if he *wasn't* a spy. It's still a strange fact that he was seen no more at the end of the war or after it was over. We shall never know. He was probably old and died, but to us, the children, he was a spy and that was that. You couldn't be too careful. This caution also applied to soldiers on manoeuvres in fields and ditches. I used to stay with Judy Freshman, a schoolfriend who lived in the next village, Wingham. (Her Father was a surgeon and later dealt with my burst appendix!) However, for now, we had enjoyable times walking with her Nanny and little brother, Roger. He was only four and we were getting on, at six, therefore we must keep anything suspicious or possibly threatening from him and soldiers going about their manoeuvres had to be very secret. We referred to them as haystacks. This could be believed as there were dozens of haystacks dotted about the fields. What seemed strange to Roger was the reverse of our subterfuge, that haystacks were soldiers and they just *weren't,* this was obvious to Roger but we persisted in the name-changing and thought we had saved the boy from any information he might have for the Germans, should they invade.

I had actually met the Freshmans because Judy and I were at this awful prep school together. Our friendship was the only positive thing to come out of that experience. When my Father and Mother first took me to "Crocksyard", a rambling old farmhouse just outside Wingham, the Headmistress, Miss Elgar, met us as the front door and was very charming. Well, she would be, wouldn't she – a few more shekels in the school's coffers. She presented me with the school hatband and explained: "The brown is for the earth; the blue is for the sky and the white for *purity.*" This last word said with the relish of one addicted to *goodness.* When I referred to *Miss Elgar*, it was because she was known by her title, her sisters were Miss Grace, Miss Marjorie and Miss Audrey. Perhaps I am being unfair to the grown-ups at the School because my main problem, horror, fear, was the bullying. When I hear what happens to children at school now I remember the awfulness of that time. I was a very shy child and not used to children in number as so many of the Ash children had been evacuated. The culprits were a group of farmers' sons who, as well as threatening and pushing and shouting, took a delight in putting spiders and other insects down my back when I was sitting in class and was afraid to react. I think this gave me my life-long difficulty with spiders, though neither then or now, would I kill one. I just regret that insects became part of the fear. I gradually discovered that if I tagged on to these boys, like I did with the Field boys when they were in Ash, I could join in as an "associate member" as it were. My first introduction to *gang culture*. For a while this worked and they stopped bullying me. They had other plans which were much more sinister. They would pick on any weakling and persuade them to come to the woods for a walk, then they would push him or her into any hollow in the trees that they could find and cover him with leaves. What ended my association with them was when they discovered barbed wire that would act as a barrier to any poor victim escaping from the "trench". Horrible. Now, I realize, that all the pictures of trench warfare or any other kind of warfare, were becoming a part of young people's lives. In the case of the *bullies*, no Grimm's fairy tales for vicarious thrills, but the distorted scenarios of being real soldiers in a real war.

The only bright spot in these troubled times for me, was cycling with my Father to another farmer's house on the way to Wingham and there being given a lift to the school at Crocksyard with the two boys of the family "Stickles". It didn't seem a funny name then and during the short car journeys I became totally captivated by the younger Stickles boy, Tony. Possibly I assumed early in life, the role of the older woman. Tony was six months younger than me. He took not the slightest notice of me but I was love-struck for the length of time I stayed at that School but the unhappiness of the situation *in* school, obliterated all other obsessions, leaving the one – I couldn't keep going to that place. When it got to the stage of locking myself in the bathroom my Mother obviously became worried. For a few days I allowed myself to be cajoled into going, but sooner rather than later, my Mother removed me and I have no idea of what she said to *Miss* Elgar. Why oh why, do we not have the courage to *tell* our parents when we are this unhappy because of *bullying*? Somewhere in our child's mind we must think it's our fault and don't want the possible consequences of admitting that.

Unconnected with the foregoing, I trust, was a persistent pain in the tummy. Dr. Fraser was called to examine me at home as I became more poorly. He felt my tummy all over, asking where the pain was. I couldn't tell him because it was *everywhere.* No-one realized that peritonitis had set in and the pain was, indeed, everywhere. My Mother then called in Judy's Father, who examined me, made the right diagnosis and my Father got out the car. It's a funny thing, that if you go to the dentist with raging toothache, it will often subside when you sit in the chair and the dentist asks which tooth is troubling you. You can't be certain. Well, the magic of Mr. Freshman's *healing hands,* as they seemed to be, had taken away the awful pain but not because I had been healed, but the appendix had burst. I was whisked into hospital in the old Austin Seven and operated on that night by Mr. Freshman. I still remember the rather unctuous nursing sister in a dark blue uniform saying: "Now we are going to paint your tummy blue." I thought she was addressing me as a *child!* I smiled along with her and was prepared for anything which would keep the pain at bay.

Anaesthetics are so much quicker and easier now. Then, having the mask put on my face, being told to count and refusing and being suffocated with Ether, was a most unpleasant experience, but I lived to tell the tale.

At home, my parents were beside themselves with worry. A burst appendix could be and often was, fatal. You don't know what your own parents go through until you have to go through similar experiences with your own children.

In hospital, I had a ward with large French windows which were protected against the bombs and the shelling by a solid brick wall. We had all got used to having views obscured, so reading was essential and a very nice nurse used to come in and give me her version of The Tale of Peter Rabbit, which included Mr. *Montgomerie* (was she being wildly patriotic?) and not *Mr. McGregor.* I thought this was very strange but I liked her, so would never have commented on her re-naming of Peter's arch-enemy. She it was, who lifted me out of bed when I was feeling a little better and took me to a sight I shall never forget – a ward full of wounded airmen, all in uniform blue pyjamas and some so swathed in bandages their faces were not visible but those that could see smiled and waved to me and I smiled and waved back, as my lovely nurse had suggested. I doubt if she intended to show me there are always those worse off than you are, though that may have been one reaction; I think she just wanted to cheer these brave boys up by taking a little child to visit them. For me this is a most moving memory.

On The Wireless

The German attacks on Leningrad begin; the RAF flies to help in its first engagement in Russia; Russians claim to have taken the outskirts of the City; 163,636 Jews still said to be living in Germany; French hostages are shot in two incidents following the death of one of their soldiers; RAF attack German naval base in Norway. Hitler's short-lived triumph as the Germans close in on Moscow; The Ark Royal is finally sunk by Italian torpedo; Japanese-U.S. relations deteriorate,, culminating in the attack on Pearl Harbour.

I suppose many hats were thrown into the air when the Americans joined the Allies and began their ferocious battles with the Japanese in the South Pacific. I think we continued to hear mostly of the War in Europe with the Germans and Axis puppet regimes. *Was Heinz's Mother still in Berlin?* The Royal Artillery, to which Heinz and Max had pledged themselves, shortly moved from the vast encampment at Durlock, which had been "sussed" by the Germans and they made quite a few attempts to bomb it. To no avail as far as we knew. It wasn't possible to go through military barriers to find out what was going on or to visit soldiers who had become our friends. Understandably. One of the attempts to obliterate the camp had resulted in a bomb landing in the orchard next to where my Father's chickens had roamed in Staple. We all went to see the damage the next day. There was an enormous crater but the bomb had exploded or I'm sure we wouldn't have been allowed anywhere near. Another bomb was dropped closer to the Camp, in a friend's market garden. This time, we were told, the bomb disposal experts had to come in as the bomb had only partially exploded. Again, there was a cavernous crater created by bombs which had miraculously – and carelessly, I imagine, from the German point of view - missed their target and the Camp remained, but apart from the need for troops in all theatres of war now, there was also the need for the soldiers to be got out of Staple.

So, we lost our friends Arthur and Eddie first, then dear, dear Heinz and Max. My Mother and Heinz kept in touch somehow and remained so until their respective deaths. It was a deep and touching friendship.

At about this time Peggy, my Father's youngest sister and, of course, my aunt, was called up. She was in the 20-30 year-old age group and unmarried therefore eligible for call-up. She joined the Land Army and stayed on the same farm throughout and after the War. She was so capable and took over the management of the farm as time went on and until she retired. She became a close friend and was indispensable in the farmer's family and working lives. She became a life-long vegetarian as a result of the unacceptable side of farming that she saw. Peggy was also a bit of a wag – whenever and wherever there was a piano in a public place, she would march up to it, open the lid with a flourish – all eyes were on her by this time – sit down and after a bit of sleeve-raising, she'd crash out the opening chords of the Tchaikovsky Piano Concerto with great aplomb and then . . . she would close the piano lid, push back the stool and resume her chat and her beer. When I was a bit older I found this really embarrassing, but then teenagers find almost *everything* embarrassing except their own behaviour!

All through my childhood I called my parents "Mummy" and "Daddy" – as did everyone that I knew. I choose now to refer to them as my Mother and Father . . . . . because the former are perceived to be unacceptably middle-class. "What's in a name, eh?"

As children, generally speaking, do not keep diaries, life tends to be spherical in shape. Childhood years go onwards and upwards but events all merge into one. Long days of sunshine, climbing trees, falling off the top of one and found hanging by my vest from the branch of another. Deep snows drifting in Winter; extensive tree-pruning; acres of yellow daffodils carpeting the orchards in the Spring; blackberrying in the Autumn and endless tidying up, ploughing and, in my Father's case, digging in preparation for the coming year. The war was an integral part of the equation. It just went on and on and so did the fear when the siren sounded, when the bombers passed over, when Canterbury, nine miles away, could be seen as a raging fire; being stopped at barbed wire barriers if your journey took you beyond the 3-mile limit. A soldier in a tin hat would emerge from a sentry box, bayoneted rifle in hand and say, in time-honoured fashion: "Halt! Who goes there?" Once, when our Welsh friend, Betty Lewis had come to stay, our car was stopped one evening and her shape was spotted on the back seat. When asked the standard question, fairly sharply, she simply responded, in her delicious Welsh accent: "It's only me, Betty Lewis from Llanelly (. . .ee)".

I used to think I would like to marry a farmer, but my Mother disabused me of this notion by telling me about Robert Chandler, a very attractive man who served on the Parish Council with her and at one meeting, a mouse ran across the floor and he lifted up his great booted foot and crushed it to death. Mother was upset; he was instantly *un*attractive and it was certainly the end of my dreams of being a farmer's wife.

Every Tuesday was market day in Sandwich, just two miles down the road, and I always went with my Father. Sometimes we'd buy plants and sometimes a few pullets. Once when I was making a great fuss of a goat, it took against my Father and butted him in the legs from behind, so he lost his balance. Oh dear. He wasn't very fond of goats anyway – the smell, apart from the butting – but I would almost invariably cuddle and kiss them and come home stinking of their particular scent! I have a vivid memory of talking to a lone calf whose ear had been clamped with its label and was still bleeding. It seemed to take a liking to me and I spent a long time with it – presumably "he" and was able to put my arms round his neck and give him a bit of heartfelt love. Thank God I didn't have to know what happened to him. I felt he had trusted me and in leaving him I had let him down.

There were so many *acts of betrayal* by me as I saw them. When people talk of *living off the land* as was imperative in wartime, it meant the life-death cycle was fairly rapid. I used to wander round, chatting to animals and birds and one day I came across an old boy called Sinclair, who lived in a wooden house at the boundary of one of our orchards and never had much to say. On this occasion, I looked through the open door of his garden shed and he was skinning a black rabbit. What I couldn't get over was that the creature's eyes seemed to be staring at me. Old Sinclair gave me a strange look, I remember and wondered why. I realized some years later that he didn't think it was a scene that a child should be witnessing. I remember the creature's eyes. We had a barnful of rabbits, who had babies, of course, and with whom I instantly formed an attachment. Even my pet rabbit, Spot, who was so soft and biddable, had to go and I had to accept that this was the order of things. Chickens had slightly less tragic lives as they produced eggs on a regular basis - perhaps for years - and chicks. In the Spring we would wake in the morning to the sound of loud cheeping. It would be the chicks having broken out of the eggs which were keeping warm in the airing cupboard. Ducks and even goslings came later but they were all enchanting and much more agreeable than an alarm clock. I had seen many chickens killed and on the whole it seemed quick and painless. However, this was not the fate of all of them and My Mother and I had some pets among them. She had Granny Grey, who was black and used to hop on to her knee when we were sitting in the garden and I had Slatey, unimaginatively named because she was, yes, *grey.* Slatey used to sit on my shoulder and we'd go visiting together. Old Mrs. Oliver, our neighbour the other side of the Magnolia trees, would welcome Slatey and me with: "Would you like a bun?" Oh yes. The *bun* was always a rock cake and I would fetch the tin from the larder and Mrs. Oliver, Slatey and I would sit down at the table and munch our rock cakes.

To end these tales of animal lives cut short, I am still haunted by the sound of pigs shrieking so that they could be heard all over the village. They were delivered by farmers – including my Father – to Mr. Foat, who slaughtered and butchered them. I find this memory still dreadfully disturbing.

Happily, Pongo, our beloved cat still, was not on anyone's death-to-eat list and tolerated endless attention from me. It is amazing that cats put up with the uncomfortable holds in which children seem to hang on to them. I still admire his tolerance. His favourite food was fish - salmon paste on little cubes of brown bread. None of your tins of cat food then.

After my unhappy experiences at Crocksyard and my appendectomy, I had a bit of time off but I think this was the long Summer holiday, after which I was allowed to go to the Kelsey School, though my Mother had always wanted to keep my education out of her jurisdiction. She even accepted my being seated next to Colin Smith, for whom I'd always had a childish fancy. He was like the other *friends* amongst boys I had known – and he was *naughty*. Rumour had it that he and his older brothers used to go down to Sandwich Bay and shoot off guns whilst avoiding barbed wire entanglement – and mines. When he grew up he became a gunsmith and much in demand by the *huntin', shootin' and fishin'* obsessives. He did remain way up on my list of lovely young men for some years though! Such hypocrisy.

Great relief from days and nights of war was *The Wireless*. I was allowed to stay up for ITMA (It's That Man Again) with Tommy Handley. This was occasionally broadcast from the Garrison Theatre in Lerwick, Shetland and in the sixties I almost felt the presence of this wonderful team when I was on tour there. ITMA was bizarre and funny enough to be an advance warning of The Goons and Monty Python. It had a mixture of gifted comedy performers, who each had one-liners that became catch-phrases for years. Then there was The Happidrome, with "Ramsbottom and Enoch . . . and Me!" as their opening and closing songs would tell us. Interspersed with the comedy was Vera Lynn and her singing of *The White Cliffs of Dover* which would bring a nationalistic tear to my eye then – and now. The news at 9.00 pm was listened to by my parents and me, every night and I understood more of the facts and their implications. *Monday Night At Eight* was another must and my Mother's favourite, probably – *The Brains Trust*. I remember this more as it continued over the years, but I did become quite attached to Professor Joad, Julian Huxley and Commander Campbell. Good programme. They should bring it back!

Meanwhile, Orson Welles produced the great *CITIZEN KANE* which I was far too young to appreciate or be taken to see then. He made his appearance in my life many years hence!

We did go to the cinema regularly. Usually we went with

Mrs. Sanders, a teaching friend of my Mother's, but on one occasion we had to go on Friday night, rather than Saturday, to see *GONE WITH THE WIND*. In those days, tea-dances were the thing – anything to occupy people's worried minds and to bring a few smiles to worried faces. On this occasion I only really remember this part of the outing as the film had been quite upsetting. My Mother having vowed never to take me to the cinema again after I had spent the whole time in the cinema crying my eyes out for *DUMBO* and we missed most of the film while Mother and I were in the Ladies', she mopping my eyes and I, inconsolably broken hearted. However, she must have thought I was grown-up enough now, at seven years old. I digress. On the Friday of our visit to see Gone With The Wind, we went as usual to the tea room for a cuppa and a Chelsea bun – very popular, sort of twirly and with shiny sugar on top and currants inside. Don't know if anyone bakes them now. In the tea-room I was seated near to the dance floor and my parents danced. I was a bit jealous! The song I will never forget was *Don't Sit Under The Apple Tree With Anyone Else But Me*. This tea-time is so vivid in my memory and the song always brings a tear to the eye. The next night, Saturday, Mrs. Sanders, who would have been with us, went to the film and the cinema – The Regal – was bombed. Mrs. Sanders regaled us with the tale of how she dived under a table in the tea-room and saw a great mirror crashing down towards her, hitting the table under which she was hiding. *Gone,* indeed, with the *Wind of Warfare* and *gone* might we have been, had we not gone on Friday but our usual day, Saturday.

Whilst it had been reassuring to see my parents holding each other and smiling, I still dreaded another row. One night after I had gone to bed, as usual, wide awake and waiting for the bombers to fly over. (I used to block my ears with my fists but could never obliterate the sound and I can still hear them through covered-up ears, now.) I could hear my parents having an argument and I really don't know what it was about. I just heard my Mother announce that she was going to *LEAVE THIS HOUSE* and the door slammed. I ran down the stairs and out through the back door. My Father, oddly, didn't follow or deter me. There was Mother, striding out down the long grass path between the orchards at the back of the house. She had got to the small delapidated garden-tool shed half way towards her little garden on the boundary hedge between us and Mr. Benbow's hop-garden when I caught up with her and clasped her hand tightly. She responded calmly and to a certain extent reassured me that she was not, in fact, going to "leave this house", but for me it was an introduction to a unique fear that so many children have, that their parents *might* just leave them.

On a more nationally significant front – my Uncle John was Dean of the Faculty of Arts at St. Andrew's University He was a highly respected philosopher with a keen interest in those activities connected with the war and with which he was involved. Uncle John was called upon to be one of the interviewers of Rudolf Hess, Hitler's right hand man, who landed in Scotland to *seek a peace solution* apparently with the full approval of Hitler and the terms were, from Uncle John's point of view, ridiculous but if you were German and enjoying the success that Germany was enjoying still, in 1942 - we were "beaten" and they were being utterly reasonable. All sorts of promises were contained in the document about how *respected* Great Britain would be, how it would never be invaded if we just signed on the dotted line. Our Empire was another matter. They wanted access to every area of that and, of course, would have won the war very quickly if they had had that access. I do ask the question now – how many amongst us were in total sympathy with Oswald Mosley's point of view and who may well have led Hitler to believe that all he had to do was send Herr Hess over with all these *reasonable* suggestions and Great Britain would be his friend and supporter for life. *No names, no pack-drill.* Well, the V.I.Ps and Uncle John declined and Hess returned to Germany with that message. Of course, it was a long time before we heard all this.

On our visits to St. Andrews my Mother and my Uncle would sit up late and talk for hours. The house was too big and sprawling for me to eavesdrop in those days. Maybe I slept better. The war seemed a long way away. My Mother used to say John only asked us there to be with the children when Florencia was away, or he was away and Florencia needed company. She had developed early arthritis and became more and more restricted in her activities. She was, it has to be said, a terrible snob, hence Mother's assumption that the Family Rye was welcomed out of need, rather than joy. We'll never know.

At this time the course of the war had still not turned our way and I became acutely aware of the wounded soldiers. Apart from my hospital visit, I once watched from the bridge a train (The famous *Mallard*) pulling into the station at Ryhope, a few stops further South than Newcastle, when I was staying with Granny and Aunty Lily. The train was carrying hundreds of wounded soldiers, mostly on stretchers. Ryhope Infirmary was apparently given over to war casualties but the sight of them all was a sharp reminder of the sacrifices that were being made in this war which seemed to be going on and on. *Was* going on and on.

Our beloved chickens had already had unpleasant and in a lot of cases, fatal experiences with foxes, whose point of view I have always tried to understand as I know they must kill and carry back to their dens as many fresh kills as possible to feed their families and bury the excess for later;

however, my Father was not of that opinion at all and kept making their sheds and fences more and more secure. One night there was an incendiary bomb raid which created havoc and a fate worse than death by fox, as the main cluster of bombs fell on or around the chicken sheds and in the wire-netting enclosure. Friends appeared from everywhere to try and put out the fire and rescue the *girls* as my Father used affectionately to call them. As usual, I was in bed, but awake and watching the activity from my bedroom window and being tormented by the thought of those poor chickens that didn't manage to get out of harm's way. As when my Father had his adventure sheltering under the tree next to the victim of a German fighter's machine gun, war was closer than you might think.

New kilt and Pongo above.

A Kentish Winter.

Hilda and Ann in Kensington Gardens, 1944

With uncle John.

Friends with Michael, after the pond incident!

As The Doctor – first acting role, 1944/45.

The Maltese Cross

RAF begins bombing raids on ship building ports in Germany; Quisling betrays his fellow Norwegians to the Nazis; Malta is attacked - over 2000 raids - and our rescue forces are bombed and in some cases, annihilated. The brave people of Malta were awarded the George Cross. The price of petrol is increased by a penny. The Japanese bomb Ceylon and the U.S. bombs Tokyo; The Russians foil the Nazi attack; Rommel's offensive in the Desert drives the allies back; Eisenhower is appointed to lead U.S. forces in Europe; Montgomery takes over the 8th Army in the Desert. Britain signs a 20-year pact with Russia and the U.S. engage in the ferocious Battle of Midway.

Amongst the rescue forces referred to was H.M.S. Manxman and Albert describes the fears and losses of all concerned in trying to relieve Malta. Albert himself, in the midst of bombing and torpedoeing, expresses the admiration of the brave Maltese people and how urgently all of the ships' crews felt the need to supply them with food and fuel.

Apart from Malta, whose fate was in the balance and a particular magazine showed alarming and dramatic pictures, I doubt if I was aware of these historic disasters and/or victories but all the grown-ups I knew kept stiff upper lips and smiles – if both are possible simultaneously. People remained positive and so, in between the frightened times, we children laughed and played, got into mischief and roamed in the fields and the woods. Skipped to the baker for bread, Vye's for the groceries, Bickers for the newspapers and sweet ration; Mr. Clugston for our medicines. His shop was a mysterious yet orderly place. Walls covered with wooden drawers where pills, potions and bandaging were kept and shelves on which were bottles and jars with pills and liquid medicines for coughs, indigestion, influenza and probably heart failure. All cures came out of Mr. Clugston's bottles and drawers.

John Foat, the butcher, by this time always had the reminder for me of sawdust and Heinz's Mother's starvation diet. Also, Miss Holman, who sat in a minute "office" in the corner of the shop and who we were later told, was having an affair with Mr. Foat. Hard to imagine the two of them, one very sweet but "getting on" and the other, short, fat and a little overbearing. Anyway, that's what they were up to and that was another reason to exercise a vivid imagination. No wonder Mrs. Foat always seemed to be *cross*. We children, including her own grandchildren, were actually afraid of her. We were banned from so many places where we liked to play, including the empty garage where we were being taught to tap-dance by a visiting friend of one of the older girls. I could only do that with my right foot and that remains the case, though years hence, on stage, I would have to *look* as though I knew exactly what I was doing and how I was doing it! Back to Mrs. Foat for a minute. She was prone to malapropisms. One day, Mother and I bumped into her in the village street and they began discussing jam-making – a major occupation in war-time – and Mrs. Foat said: "We don't 'ardly eat no jam now Jack's gawn away (*to war*). We're very ab-ste-menious." My Mother squeezed my hand very hard but it did become a source of amusement for the Family. It might seem a little cruel now, but if she'd only been *nicer* . . . and less pre*tentious*.

Ash had its own RADAR station. We didn't know that these places were scattered all round the South-East coast from 1937. We knew something was going on at the top of Ringleton Park, the other side of the wooded hill. We used to cycle up there and sometimes visit my cousins who had a farm the other side of Ringleton. There was an odd-shaped pony who didn't know he was odd-shaped and he had an ever-present companion who was a sheep. They were inseparable and both willing to be stroked and talked to by us. Well, me anyway, the boys weren't too keen then on all those *physical* displays of affection.

Over the period of time that we cycled to Ringleton, we observed the steady excavation *inside* the hill. It seemed very slow and when it was eventually unaccompanied by builders, there seemed little sign of any alteration to the natural order of the hillside – except a tall tower with many cables and something that went round and round and back and forth on top of the mast. Later, we observed various "slits" in the hillside which we found significant – who was inside the hill? A family friend, George Hills, was in the Observer

Corps which was a very responsible occupation and only he seemed to be allowed near this now secret place and he, of course, wasn't allowed to say, or just didn't! He had been a young soldier in the First World War and I do believe would have lied about his age to be an active part of the Second World War. So, yes, he took his responsibilities very seriously and bore them with pride.

Most of my Father's brothers were in reserved occupations, so didn't fight in foreign parts, apart from Sam (Cyril, really. Everyone in the family called him or her self by names other than their own.) Sam, who was endearing but always a bit mad, was apparently careering about France on his motorbike ferrying messages to and from different units and taking terrible risks. He was *mentioned in dispatches.* Very impressive. When I married Andrew, a long time hence, he and Sam started talking about their experiences in France towards the end of the war and it has to be said that at that time they were being a bit naughty. Andrew was gathering bottles of whisky left behind by the enemy and passing them along the line. This, apparently was precisely *the line* that

Sam's regular trips had taken him and all those years later, they believed they must have been in business together. Andrew being the hunter-gatherer and Sam the deliverer. Doubtless money changed hands!

Albert Pettman, meanwhile, had a gift for writing poetry – as many discovered they did, I believe. The poetry he wrote for his beloved Nora, was moving and beautiful and written throughout engagements of war, alongside his Journals. She had always known that he had this sensitive and truly loving nature. She treasured that poetry on those scrappy bits of paper but didn't share them with us until after his death, many years later.

Albert was Mentioned in Dispatches in The London Gazette on January 1st, 1943. for his bravery in striving to rescue his fellow sailors after H.M.S. Manxman had been torpedoed.

In 1943-44 the war on all fronts started to turn the Allies' way though horrors were still to be disclosed.

The Jews in Warsaw
Rachmaninoff Dies

Jews slaughtered in Warsaw ghetto; Stalingrad is defended & Germans routed; Monty triumphs at El Alamein; Welfare State proposed; British war films – Coward's IN WHICH WE SERVE; Humphrey Jennings's documentaries including FIRES WERE STARTED – a portrait of the Blitz and TARGET FOR TONIGHT; then THE FIRST OF THE FEW, the story of Mitchell, the designer of the Spitfire. In America CASABLANCA. Germans surrender Stalingrad; first day-time bombing of Berlin; Italians driven out of Tripoli by the British; Rachmaninov dies; mass grave of Polish officers found; the dam busters raid devastated Ruhr and Eder valleys and two large dams breached;. Jews chased through Warsaw sewers; tide turns in U-Boat war; Mussolini deposed; French Resistance chief, Jean Moulin, tortured and executed; Allies attack major German weapons base at Peenemunde; Italy signs an armistice; Italy declares war on Germany; Bevin Boys are called up to work down the mines; Glenn Miller's band plays and records for troops; the song LILLI MARLENE, formerly the Germans' nightly morale-booster to their troops, becomes the province of the English-speakers, sung by Marlene Dietrich; Lorenz Hart and . . . Fats Waller die. DNA is discovered to be solution to mystery of gene characteristics; The Siege of Leningrad is broken.

Details of allied victories were coming in thick and fast and a spirit of optimism lifted worry from the grown-ups' faces. However, the raids did continue, though to a lesser extent and the retreat under-stairs was still necessary.

By this time I had been sent to the preparatory department of the Simon Langton School for Girls, in Canterbury. The School had been evacuated from the centre of the City, into a large, sprawling red-brick building which had been an asylum. I don't think this worried any of the children as we probably didn't understand the implications. I was more concerned with going amongst strange people and my shyness was still a barrier. However, the *girls* were very pleasant, as were the teachers. On one occasion we broke one of the rules about going into certain small rooms in the place. We found ourselves in a rectangular space, with a high, barred window and walls padded with stuffed white leather. My first and so far last, experience of a padded cell!

Canterbury is nine miles from where we lived in Ash and the long bus journey was cold and often damp. I began to suffer with muscular rheumatism. This was discovered after a dramatic evening in the City. My friends and I had caught a bus outside the School which took us into Canterbury. We got off the bus halfway down the main street – St. Peter's Street. It was raining and whilst the temptation of buying ice-creams at Di Marco's was hastening our step, I got off the pavement to get to the Westgate Towers' bus station and get home. I've always been in a hurry and the habit has stayed with me, unfortunately but not as unfortunately as that day, when, in half-light (no street lighting, remember) the double-decker bus coming up behind me didn't see me walking, as I was, in the gutter and lifted me on its enormous mudguard for several yards before I was able to slide off, avoid its great wheels and deposit myself back on the pavement. The girls were panicking but my panic was how *angry* my Mother was going to be *if she should get to hear of the episode.* I wasn't going to tell her but, well and truly shaken, walked on. Quite when we heard the air-raid siren I don't know. I remember being directed by A.R.P. wardens and soldiers from the Regiment of the Buffs, whose barracks were at the top of St. Martin's Hill, near our School and ushered at a fairly fast pace down Watling Street towards the Cathedral. At the main doors a strange figure in a flowing red gown greeted us. This was the famous – and in some people's minds – infamous, Red Dean, Dr. Hewlett Johnson. We didn't know that immediately. He ushered us, with help from a couple of Church wardens, down the worn stone steps to the crypt. There we were given cups of tea and could just about hear the sound of engines overhead and the thuds of bombs as they dropped. The Dean, it has to be said, was kind and protective. He amused us with tales of Cathedral life when things went wrong and succeeded in taking our minds off what was going on above. *Jerry* had had a few goes at the Cathedral but had not succeeded in destroying the building we all loved – yet. I don't remember the fear. I think we all felt *safe* in this vast underground haven. It didn't cross our minds that the place was full of long-since buried V.I.Ps with their statues lying in state on top of their tombs. My anxiety was – how would my parents know where I was? I don't know to this day, how they did! Eventually the all-clear went and we were taken back to the ground floor of the Cathedral through the great main doors and thence to the bus station.

I became quite ill after this episode and muscular rheumatism affecting the spine had been diagnosed. It really was a painful time and it was then, I think, that my Mother made up her mind that the travelling in the war-time conditions would have to stop and that boarding school might become an option. I soldiered on and the pain came and went. First taste of fallibility, perhaps?

When it was considered safe again, some days later, my Mother took me to Canterbury and into the Cathedral. We went through the beautiful cloisters and made our way towards the library. I remember the steps that led up to it disappeared half way up. I'm sure we shouldn't have been there but my Mother was nothing if not purposeful. The Library was in ruins. I wonder now if the books were buried and eventually saved. Long after the war we had re-visited the place and all was in order – the steps, the Library, its walls and its bookcases. Now, however, this was quite a shock. How lucky we had been, sheltering in the crypt and that the bombs had missed the main body of the Cathedral.

I told my Mother that the Dean had been very kind to us and she explained that people found his politics suspect. He was openly Communist and that meant that he was on the side of the Russians and who knew what their intentions were? In future, I noticed, the Archbishop would sit on one side of the congregation and the Dean on the other. Maybe they would have anyway?

That may well have been my last war-related experience had it not been for the sinister appearance of the "doodle bug".

Doodle-bugs

Orde Wingate, hero of Burma, is killed; Victorious Red Army powers through the Crimea; Invasion plans turn UK into armed camp; de Gaulle appointed head of French forces; American forces launch Pacific assault; first prefabricated house is ready: 5,000,000 more promised; the Battle of Monte Cassino breaks the German spine; Rome is liberated by Allies; US bombers reach Japanese mainland; Rommel prepares to counter Allied plans to invade Europe; Hungarian Jews face new Nazi threat; "Miracle Weapon" threatens London.

Well, the miracle weapon, which became known as the doodle-bug, didn't just threaten London. Some eerily flew across our green fields and we would run out, looking upwards and hearing a noise like a tractor. While you were hearing them, that was o.k. When the sound stopped, they were going to behave like very powerful rockets which, of course, is what they were. I'm still reminded of witnessing the sight and sound of these when an aircraft flying overhead seems to have a strange engine noise. I wait for the sound to stop . . . just in case it does. Frightening times, those were.

The War was still months away from ending – and then, only ending in Europe. Ferocious fighting continued and not all of it reported on our nightly news programme. *We had to keep positive* so we did.

D-DAY: ALLIED TROOPS STORM ASHORE IN NORMANDY.

Percy Andrews - later married to my Aunt's beloved housekeeper, and whom we all knew behind the counter at the hardware shop in Ash – was on one of the first landings, managed to get off the beach and follow his instructions to head for a mansion some miles from the coast at the edge of the Ardennes, where his unit would be reassembled. Percy and his pal reached the outer walls of the place and Percy, who wasn't very tall, pulled himself up to look over the wall and see if it was clear to proceed across the meadow the other side. His six fellow soldiers had all been killed. A sniper got Percy in the chest at this moment. Apparently it was a serious wound and he took a long while recovering. As a reward for his bravery – or folly – he was returned to his Unit whose designation was to effect the release of prisoners in *BELSEN*. That was Percy's last war experience and by far the most horrific and haunting in his mind. He didn't talk about it much and after the war until his recent death, he returned to join his erstwhile comrades as they gathered every year on the Beaches of Normandy.

Back to childhood - Village life continued much as usual. I would walk down the Street, as often as not, holding either My Mother's hand or my Father's. I took this lovely man's part in my life rather for granted. He was always *there*, I could always find him working away, often erecting fencing for more chickens and geese, digging, pruning, picking fruit. His strength and the strength of his love has lasted my lifetime. So many happy memories – he made a little garden for me to grow flowers of my own, as he had for my Mother; he took me with him when he visited other farms; sometimes for a new set of pullets, Rhode Island Reds and Light Sussex usually. Once, he said he was going to fetch some goslings. My experience of these little fluffy creatures was from the cheeping noises that came from the linen cupboard when they were hatching, so I leapt at the chance of being able to cuddle lots of them on our return journey.

This trip was to the Beans. *Uncle* Bean was my paternal grandmother's brother and he kept, amongst other creatures, bees. These fascinated me and I would follow him in and out of the garden of hives, intrigued by the amazing organisation of the bee. Uncle Bean had no fear of them. He loved them all and so I did, too. One day, to show us how *tame* they were, he let a bee fly into his open mouth, closed his lips for a few seconds, then opened them and out would fly the bee, completely unperturbed by the experience, presumably because it had all happened before. This sounds like a tall story but is actually true. Amazing, but gave me my love of these clever and endearing little creatures.

Back to the goslings. We followed Uncle Bean to a shed at the back of the garden and my Father told me I could carry them if I wanted to. Alas, nobody had told me that they were a few months old, very large and pretty panic-stricken. I remember trying to hold on to two of them, one under each arm while they *relieved* themselves down my new dress and that bothered me more than the geese who were fighting me for supremacy. What was I going to say to my Mother about the mess on the frock so recently purchased from Aunty Ida Harden? Between the three of us we got the rest of the *goslings* into a big box in the back of the car and we let them out into their own house in the chicken run which was large enough in area for them never to meet. Of course, they did and they, the geese, acted as protectors to the chickens and, as I learned, are the best watch-dogs anyone can possibly own.

Subsequent visits to the Beans were always joyous for me. They had eight dogs, all of whom had complete freedom and the Beans lived amongst fields and woods, so they could come and go as they please. There were no sheep in the surrounding fields, just corn, potatoes, sugar beet and fruit trees. The oldest member of the dog family was Peggy; she was twenty-two and slept her life away in the warmest possible spot – in the hearth of the great open-range cooker. I loved all the canine family and the Beans themselves were lovely, kind people. Characteristic, in fact, of anyone in my Father's family.

I had in those days, thirty-four first cousins. They were all over the country, the wealthier ones being the larger-scale farmers who inherited well! There were aunts and uncles and cousins in all the neighbouring villages and we, my Father and I, continued to visit them often. There was always a welcome, a cuppa and something grown in the garden. All our lives centred at that time on what grew and/or was reared. Rationing, it has to be said, did not bother us unduly. I remember an enormous stone pot in which the eggs were placed and covered in something called water-glass. In that state the eggs lasted all through Winter. One of my discoveries was powdered egg when I stayed with one of my friends in Ramsgate; *then* I realized how blessed we were.

There are many things for an only child to do and providing there is someone, somewhere in the house, the world is your oyster. It certainly was mine and of course talking to the animals, mine or those I visited – Molly, Mr. Foat's horse and Peter Harden who was a wire-haired terrier and a favourite with everybody. He belonged to John Harden, Aunty Ida and Uncle Bertie's son – he with the *intelligence* to be in the Intelligence Corps. John was away so much that Peter frequently stayed with John's parents Ida and Bertie. Peter just loved to be loved and he loved to do tricks. He was instantly obedient – I suspect John was a bit of a control-freak – Peter would catch biscuits from a great height; jump over an obstacle course in the garden, immaculately. When I was allowed to go down the Street on my own, Peter would be one of my first calls and what a welcome there was!

If it was raining or too cold to go out, I would arrange all the chairs in the drawing room and two or three from the dining room, into the sections of the orchestra. I had always imagined where the players were when I listened to music on the radio, but I expect my Mother had told me, especially since I embarked on my "conducting" adventure. We had an old wind-up gramophone and loads of seventy-eight records. I played and played them, everything from pop songs of the day like "Me and Jane In A Plane" to Schubert's Unfinished Symphony which I loved and really had quite a deep appreciation of the music and its construction. Other favourites were "In A Monastery Garden" and "In A Persian Market" by Ketelby. My orchestra must have got bored stiff with these last two as I waved Grandfather Wright's baton at them from my *rostrum -,* the pouffe from the fireside rug on which it was actually rather difficult to keep balanced. The conductor fell off her rostrum a few times. It was all so enjoyable and utterly absorbing. Other memorable pieces were The Lark Ascending and A Walk Through Paradise Garden – the latter, forever in my mind associated with the walled garden at the Peppers.

It's a strange juxtaposition with the war ever-present at the same time as what would otherwise be an idyllic childhood in a beautiful part of the Country. The Garden of England indeed. But the war is still going on.

Nazi Death Camps

Mass evacuation as V-1s fall on London; Hitler escapes bomb assassination attempt. Truman to be FDR's running mate in U.S.; French tanks lead Allies into Paris; second front opened by Allies in France; Nazi death camps found in Poland and Nazi tanks raze Warsaw.

So, we were getting there as 1944 approached 1945 and I was reaching my tenth birthday. Still at the Simon Langton School and enjoying close friendships with three friends in my form, I also burst upon the drama scene. It never ceases to amaze me that people as horribly shy as I was, actually get up on a stage and face large numbers of people and *enjoy* it. My Mother had written me a sketch called "The Doctor" and I was he! I was dressed in a tail coat, pin-striped trousers and a top hat. I was also given a pince-nez with a long handle. This became the first of many props I have found invaluable in my years on the stage. When in doubt, play with it, put it down and pretend to lose it; wave it about hysterically or use it imperiously to emphasize or illustrate a point I remember the laughs coming at me from the audience of girls and teachers alike.

It was the most exhilarating time I'd ever known. The secret is, of course, that you're not *you*. The character gets the laughs, draws the tears and carries all the responsibility for the person being someone else on the stage. Although I had provided *entertainment* every Christmas for the Family, using funny accents (again – not *me*) and singing songs of the moment, this was different, this was the beginning of a life-long love of the stage.

Macarthur's Return

MacArthur keeps his promise and returns to the Philippines; Germans on the run throughout Europe; Rommel chooses an honourable death; Paras cut off at Arnheim.

The involvement with my *orchestra* continued and it was clear, if not entirely to me, that music and theatre were a part of me – and a very *happy* part of me.

I had started to learn the piano when I was six and loved to play. My first teacher was Miss Veitch, who lived in Canterbury but she was peripatetic in her little box-like Austin 7. She drove round to all her pupils' houses - *and* this may have influenced my affection for Miss Veitch – she travelled her three cats with her wherever she went. She made us give mini-concerts regularly in her drawing room. These were a bit nerve-wracking but my playing seemed to pass muster. The only criticsm I have now of Miss Veitch's teaching is that she kept covering my hands to make me look at the music. Rightly or wrongly I always blamed her for making me a better sight-reader than a memorizer. Once my eyes were forced on to the page, eliciting the sound from my hands alone became much more difficult. Years and years later I realized that if you practised enough *with* the music, it became so familiar that it actually entered the memory bank and you could perform without looking at the music. The same goes for learning lines, I later found. You *photographed* them, however many times each page took – no more than three on a good day! That the repetition of the lines would remove your mind from the page and even referring to it, particularly on a *first night*, was disconcerting.

Anyway, that's where my love of music began and thankfully, has increased throughout my life.

Evening games with Alice and Annie Laming continued and got a bit more grown-up. The card game – "Lexicon" became a great favourite and was an early introduction to Scrabble, to which I have been addicted ever since.

Walking down the Street one day, holding my Father's

hand, as ever, a local farmer greeted us. He was accompanied by a nice looking young man in the uniform of a German prisoner of war. He smiled and offered his hand to me in which he had a fig. I hid behind my Father and to this day I'm concerned that he thought it was because he was a German. In fact, I really didn't like figs! Why didn't I say that? Gauche as usual.

Apparently farmers who employed p.o.ws preferred the Germans as they didn't mind hard work. Easier than on the Russian Front I imagine. The Italians were less industrious, though if you ever get a chance to see the amazing and beautiful little church they built from a Nissen hut, on the edge of Scapa Flow in the Orkney Islands, you would admire their hard work and artistry. It was constructed with love and I feel sure gave these young men the feeling that home was not so far away, even in the sometimes cold and inclement weather with which this part of the British Isles is very familiar.

The Ardennes

Allies take first city in the Fatherland; Red Army and Tito capture Belgrade; Hitler forms Home Guard for Germany; The war is over for our Home Guard; British land in Greece; RAF bombers sink German ship, Tirpitz; FDR is US president for the fourth time; Patton's tanks roll into the strategically vital region, the Sarrland; Ardennes breakout surprises Allies; Glenn Miller goes missing over Channel; Golden Age dawns on London stage with Richardson and Olivier.

So, it was still going on, this hideous war, but the end did seem to be in sight. We were all wondering when Uncle Bill would return from North Africa. Alas, in January 1945, Granny Wright died so she never saw her beloved second son again. He returned six months later and stayed with us briefly on his way from Dover to Durham. He looked very handsome, I thought, in his officer's uniform and his padre's collar.

Whilst there had been an amusing side to Uncle Sam's war – Sam would never say *why* he had been mentioned in dispatches and none of the family ever found out and anyway, at the time he and my husband, Andrew, were possibly engaged in the same nefarious activities with bottles of whisky left by the retreating Germans, we smiled, rather than wept, at their respective predicaments at the time in Northern France.

Where there is comedy however, there is always pathos and Uncle Bill's story fell into this category, not in any way comparable with Albert Pettman's uniquely frightening and courageous times. Though I knew nothing of what Bill and my Mother were talking about in that brief time with us in 1945. I was told, with sadness, by my Mother, years later.

Apparently Uncle Bill, the Padre, stationed in Eritrea, had spent much time praying over the sick, trying to reconcile his religious restrictions with the great desire to pick up a gun and shoot all those responsible for *his* soldiers' deaths. While spending so much of his time with the sick and dying he developed a friendship with one of the nurses which deepened into love – whether or not an affair, I don't know, such descriptions were not used, certainly by my Mother, or indeed by most people in those days, but this was a love that he had not felt before. When he married my Aunt, Mary Mackenzie, it was considered a *suitable* marriage and Granny Wright had encouraged it. Mary, on her part, adored Bill and was loyal and good to him – and able to call on her family's money and this was one of the problems in their marriage. Later on, it was Mary who insisted on the private schools to which the children, my cousins Angus and Alison went. Bill, on a parson's salary and some misgivings about money and privilege, eventually agreed but was never happy about it. So, back to his war - there he was, a long way from home, in a hot and hostile country, finding the kind of love he himself had not known. Added to the guilt he had felt about betraying his wife, he was also, as he saw it, betraying his dog-collar. When he stopped with us it may well have been his desire to tell his sister Hilda all and delay by a few days, his return to Mary and his responsibilities in Durham.

I used to go and stay with my cousins when Uncle Bill was Rector of Brancepeth. We had good times, riding the pony, Darkie, in the Castle grounds. There was nothing politically incorrect about his name, he was indeed *a dark horse*! Other outings would include being taken by Mary's mother, who was a volunteer in the W.V.S., to visit miners in their little cottages and most of them had much loved greyhounds or whippets. These were happy visits. At home, in Brancepeth, however, it was obvious that all was not well.Mary and Bill never had any *conversations;* he had a separate bedroom. He delivered the parish magazines on Darkie, would not use "Mary's car" and would travel on the bus to and from Durham and usually took the dog, aptly named "Scamp", with him Uncle Bill lived up to his reputation as an absent-minded cleric when on more than one occasion, he forgot that he'd taken the dog and it would travel to and from Durham, tied to the seat in front. Thankfully, the drivers and conductors knew him and would ring Mary up she would then go in the car and fetch the dog, who hadn't suffered at all because everyone at the bus terminal knew and loved him.

Bill was indeed absent-minded in that his thoughts were elsewhere with the woman he had grown to love. They communicated by letter and this kept him going until one day Mary said, quite out-of-the-blue: "Hadn't this better stop??" He didn't know that she was aware of these exchanges but he did what he felt he had to do and ended what remained of the love affair. It seemed to all of us that he never recovered from the heartbreak and indeed, not long afterwards, he sat in an armchair, revising the sermon he had just finished writing for the Sunday to come, closed his eyes for a little sleep and his heart did break. At any rate, it stopped. That then was the end of a rather sad life.

His earlier years had been spent in the shadow of his brother, my Uncle John, who seemed to excel in whatever academic challenges he took on. It has to be said that Mary loved Bill till the day she died but they were both, in different ways, victims of the times into which they were born.

Lloyd George Dies

Ring roads planned for a new London; Civil war grips Greece; The Queen thanks women for their war work; Allies roll back the Ardennes offensive; food riots break out in Berlin as civilians dig trenches; Dresden devastated – 130,000 killed; Allied forces close in on Berlin; American Marines raise the flag on Iwo Jima; US Seventh Army crosses the Rhine; "Werewolves" kill German collaborators; Communists take over in Balkans; Lloyd George dies at 72.

Now that I had reached the grand old age of ten, I could follow most of the News and realize that it "wouldn't be long now". The other ten-year-old who died was our beloved cat, Pongo. He was a long-haired Persian, meticulous about keeping himself clean, but had over the years swallowed too much hair and one of the infamous hairballs developed inside him and made him very ill and the locum vet was unable to save him. Later, when Major Gallie, the boss, returned from holiday, he told us he could have saved Pongo. Fat lot of good that was. I was more inconsolable at the cat's death than I had been about my Grandmother's, two months earlier. It has happened subsequently that my grief over the loss of an animal has exceeded the grief over human deaths. I do believe that one sparks off the other. The stiff upper lip that you keep when a *grown-up* dies is because you think you are supposed to *be* grown up. There are no such constraints when a pet dies and all the sorrows come together.

End of The Reich

Reich's final days: Allies in Berlin; Allied prisoners reveal horrors of the German camps; A glimpse into Hell as Nazi death camps fall; Roosevelt dies on the eve of victory; "United Nations" is born in San Fransisco; Vienna is liberated with buildings intact; Il Duce is shot then strung up by his heels; Germans in Italy surrender to the Allies; THE FUEHRER KILLS HIMSELF; Germans are weary, hungry and crushed; Britain resounds to victory celebrations.

Our beloved village Home Guard marched proudly into the Street, in lines of three, in the first of which was my Father. Well, he was tall, dark and handsome and rhythmical which, alas, could not be said of all of his comrades whose co-ordination between feet, arms and gun was not always suited to marching. What did that matter? The war was over. We didn't yet know the detailed horrors of the concentration camps; didn't know the story of Anne Frank and the Six Million Jewish people. Of course war wasn't over in the Far East and the shocking tales from those prison camps were yet to be told.

The Atom bomb had yet to be dropped. Many argued that fighting in mainland Japan would have killed far more soldiers and civilians than did the Bomb. The jury's still out on that one, though most of us suspect that while this was probably the case the history of and devastation *because* of, the bomb, changed the world. At the time, I do believe most people were relieved that two months after war ended in Europe, it came to a dubious conclusion in Japan.

In Ash, I don't remember any signs of euphoria. People worked hard as they had done for the last six years. There were, however, no raids to worry about, no thuds of bombs falling and no enemy aircraft overhead. Whenever there was a thunderstorm, my Mother said, with even more conviction, that was indeed God having the last word.

Biggest disappointment – bananas! I'd no idea what a banana was, but people had talked longingly of the day they could have a banana again. We were sitting in the car, which was now off the blocks on which it had been forced to reside when petrol was increasingly in such short supply. Happily, it was capable of being driven again. My Father turned to me in the back seat and said: "There – you have your first taste of a banana." He said it as though it was an accomplishment. I'm afraid, with extreme ingratitude, I spat it out. Alien taste; the first of many that the war had kept from us.

Now, in my mind, memory and dreams, I walk the village street, on the way stroking Major Gallie's Scots terrier – who was one of only three dogs that have ever tried to bite me, so I don't know why I flatter him by dreaming about him. On past the mysterious house, shrouded in trees and shrubs and in a state of disrepair that had belonged to Mrs. Vining. She had once summoned my Father to help her remove an Old English sheepdog that had crawled into her kitchen and died under the table. She herself went that way not long after though not under the table. The two events are not, I think, connected.

I pass another lugubrious home, that of the Hogbins. They were a family of auctioneers but the brother, Leslie, was a retired vet. He and two sisters lived in the house all their lives and when Leslie died, the two devoted sisters kept everything that was his, exactly as it had been, from his clothes hanging in the wardrobe, his handkerchieves neatly ironed and folded and his pipe still in his ash tray. A long time hence my dog, Kelpie, refused to cross the threshold of that house; the only time I had known her to refuse entering *any*one's house if we did so. To the dog this was a haunted house.

Mr. Foat and Miss Holman are still in their unusual alliance in his butcher's shop and Mrs. Foat, grim-faced as ever, will be in her garden, telling us to stop kicking the football into her flower beds

The Draysons live across the road from there, getting very old now. My friend and fish-pond torturer, Michael, once kicked a football through her pantry window which landed in a plate of ham. I was mortified but the old girl took it all in her shaky stride. Old Drayson, as he was known, could be a bit tricky and waved his stick a lot, in anger, so a football through a window was an exciting change for him perhaps from scaring the birds off his strawberry plantation.

And there are the Armstrongs, the Lamings *would you like a game?* I can hear Annie saying. Oh yes – I would. Then a nice lady called Mrs. Herrington and her daughter, Barbara.

Next, I pass Jacobs, the hardware store, with Percy the D-Day veteran, beavering away fetching and carrying and reaching up to shelves, pouring paraffin into cans the customers had brought for the purpose. Always polite, as was the Family Jacobs. Granny Jacobs in her nineties and long black dresses at all times. I loved that shop.

I drop in to the paper shop and steer clear of Mrs. Bicker who was always up for a fight – papers were delivered – no they were not – well the bill stands . . . No penny-cornets any more – and no twenty Craven A for my Mother at two and four pence, which had always left change for the ice-cream.

The last place I shall enjoy remembering and reliving is the Hardens' shop and home. We spent so much time there. I can see Ida trying to sell my mother Utility vests for me and Bertie offering me a little box of "snitch-wipers". Kind, kind people.

I won't float up to Guilton where the old forge used to be, nor will I peer in the window of the Miss Burtons' cottage and watch them mend, make and embroider, mend make and . . . I won't retrace my steps up Molland Lane or Chequer Lane. Each road led to the hamlets around Ash, to some of the splendid old houses, made less so by the Army, who requisitioned them and left a bit of a mess behind. Short notice of a call to arms, perhaps.

I'll go on, past the Hardens' house, to the Meadows below the churchyard, climb over the stile into the cornfield and then, my greatest joy, the hop garden that stretched nearly as far as our own orchards. I will smell the glorious and unique smell of the hops, look right towards the oast house and then back again to the Church, still standing with its tall spire, having served an accidental purpose guiding the enemy's aircraft inland. Now I don't have to think of that. I will just look round me and tears will come into my eyes as I take in the beauty of the village and its people. My village.

These then are the childhood memories in which dwell the love of life in the country, the important and sometimes eccentric people and, of course, the animal friends. That was the beginning. Where does it go from here? Into a life of experiences so far removed from what has been described. To a future which all those in the title inhabit.

THE END

Watercolour by Frank Drew

Harden's shop prominent in the street.

CPSIA information can be obtained at www.ICGtesting.com
Printed in the USA
IOW07s1412261015
59776LV00001B/98/P

9 781909 049307